Can You Run Your Business With Blood, Sweat, and Tears? Volume I

Can You Run Your Business With Blood, Sweat, and Tears? Volume I

Blood

Stephen Elkins-Jarrett
Nick Skinner

BEP BUSINESS EXPERT PRESS

First published in 2018 by
Business Expert Press, LLC
222 East 46th Street, New York, NY 10017
www.businessexpertpress.com

ISBN-13: 978-1-63157-795-6 (paperback)
ISBN-13: 978-1-63157-796-3 (e-book)

Business Expert Press Entrepreneurship and Small Business Management Collection

Collection ISSN: 1946-5653 (print)
Collection ISSN: 1946-5661 (electronic)

Cover and interior design by S4Carlisle Publishing Services Private Ltd., Chennai, India

First edition: 2018

10 9 8 7 6 5 4 3 2 1

Printed in the United States of America.

Dedication

For Eddie and Leia

BRAND
LEADERSHIP
OPPORTUNITY
OUTCOME
DECISIONS

Abstract

What does it take to successfully lead and manage a business or a team? Management consultant and HR specialist Stephen-Elkins Jarrett and organizational development consultant Nick Skinner share their combined experience of how mastery of 15 key areas can help you drive your business, team, or even yourself to success. Presented using the acronym of BLOOD, SWEAT, and TEARS, this book, presented in three volumes, aligns some established models with common sense to give a practical view with tools and tips gained over years of working across different industries and sectors. At the heart of the book is the fascinating study of behavior, discussed through the SPECTRUM model of behavior, showing how by treating others in the way that they want to be treated, we can engage, develop, and lead them to achieve meaningful goals.

Keywords

behavior, development, HR, human resources, leadership, management, performance, SPECTRUM, strategy, team, teamwork

Contents

Foreword

Blood, Sweat, and Tears

Elkins-Jarrett & Skinner

Stephen and Nick have packed a huge amount into these three volumes. Their years of business consulting experience is evident as they make every element wholly understandable and immensely practical—this is not a book about business theory; it is a book to be put into immediate action.

Using the acronym B-L-O-O-D S-W-E-A-T-and-T-E-A-R-S, they consider 16 areas of importance in business success (the "and" is an important area, hence 16) and within these incorporate aspects as disparate as time management, presentation skills, work–life balance, vision, and performance management, in addition to the chapter titles such as Brand, Leadership, Opportunities, and so forth using illustrations from areas as diverse as Psychology and Star Wars.

Running through the book is the recurring theme of understanding and appreciating human behavior in its many facets. They expound "Spectrum" behavioral psychometric, which fits with the themes of their book—approachable, easy to understand, and practical. All other Jungian models would also work, but I agree with them that Spectrum's simplicity enhances the ability to apply the learning effortlessly and across all cultures.

Throughout the chapters, they make use of well-known, tried-and-tested theories including Tuckman, Maslow, Kotter, and Hersey & Blanchard—only models and structures that have stood the test of time rather than any that are likely to be in vogue today and forgotten tomorrow. Within these, they give their own adaptations and developments driven by decades of management consulting experience, which make them more practical and more applicable.

If you are looking for a book that covers a wide range of criteria for business success and is eminently readable, down-to-earth, practical, and developed through the crucible of decades of experience, *Blood, Sweat, and Tears* is a wise choice.

Stephen Berry

MBA, MSc, BSc(Hons), FCMA, CGMA, ACIB, DipFS, PgD

Author of *Strategies of the Serengeti* (2006; 2nd ed., 2010)

and

Teach Yourself Strategy in a Week (2012; 2nd ed., 2016)

Introduction to the Trilogy—Blood, Sweat, and Tears

"I have nothing to offer except blood, sweat and tears!" paraphrased from a speech given to the UK houses of parliament in the dark days of 1940 by Prime Minister Sir Winston Churchill.

Hello and welcome to Blood, Sweat, and Tears! Why did we write it? What is it all about? And who the heck are these guys anyway?

Stephen's Story

My story: I have been working since I was 16. My background is strange but has given me a unique insight into the commercial world that others don't get. I did not have a classic educational background. My parents divorced when I was 11. My father was in sales and my mother a sports teacher and legal secretary. At 16 my mother said leave school and go to work, we need the money. I trained as a chef, day release at Slough College, near Heathrow airport, I left after I had completed my OND and HND (Ordinary and Higher National Diplomas) to work with my father in the construction industry. I qualified in NFBPM at Diploma level. At the same time, I was involved in Amateur Dramatics. While in a play, I was approached by a director who asked me if I fancied quitting my job to be his personal assistant and learn his trade from the bottom. He was a Coopers & Lybrand Management Consultant, now running his own business. This was a single act of kindness that changed my world forever.

I went to night school to do my A levels, did a distance learning degree with UEL in Industrial Psychology—now called Organizational. Then qualified in Psychometrics, Life Coaching, NLP, CBT, did a advanced diploma in organizational psychology at Oxford learning, and then finally got my Masters in Organizational Psychology just a few years ago. Parallel to this I worked full time for Mike at Manskill Associates, watching, learning, listening, and delivering soft skill training, facilitated workshops, strategy workshops, leadership development, management, and supervisory training and coaching. I also joined the CIPD and learned everything I could about HR and worked in HR departments as an interim for some great HR directors such as Julie Sutton and Talent Directors such as Joanne Rye. I worked as an interim HR director, HR manager, employee relations manager, caseworker, a TUPE project manager, change, takeovers, mergers, and acquisitions. I saw and learned more from this strange and unusual journey through the commercial world than I would have done with a "proper job" as my wife calls it and in a traditional career along the way. I worked in the fields of catering, hospitality, healthcare, pharmaceutical, scientific institutions, and laboratories. I worked in construction, property, IT, finance, banking, FMCG, utilities, high-voltage power stations, supermarkets, motor industry, and several others, delivering soft skills training, group facilitation, coaching, team work, team building, and more. I worked in the biggest and the smallest and everything in between, and one thing remained constant for me—it is all the same. When recruiters look for someone with managerial experience in a certain industry, any manager could learn the new job and man management skills remain a constant; 80 percent is behaviors and 20 percent technical skills and knowledge and you can learn this bit as you go. Richard Branson said, "If anyone asks you if you can do this job, say yes and then learn it as you go." He has always done this.

Nick's Story

My story is almost the opposite; raised in Hertfordshire I scrapped the grades needed to do a first degree before taking a graduate job providing business and project accounting support to scientists. This was the late 1980s and the UK was still reeling from the impacts of Thatcherism, where large swaths of the UK infrastructure that had traditionally been operated using public money were being forced down a route that made them think more commercially. The reaction to the kind of externally and politically induced change created an organizational stress that taught me a lot. I realized quickly that while finance was important there was more to business than the accountants' view. Hence, I shifted away from finance and into broader business commercial management, completing an MBA with distinction in 1997 from the University of Hertfordshire and then shifting my career to London to work in the field of commercializing intellectual property, working as a business administrator for a spin-out company commercializing breakthroughs in cancer technology, developing plans for seed funds, and managing a large network of technology transfer stakeholders. Again, in this role I was providing commercial and business support to some very clever scientists. I moved back into agricultural sciences in 1999, working on business plans and change programs in that sphere for the next 13 years. It was a long time, but there were so many projects and exciting new businesses being developed that it was really more like four or five different jobs. Certainly, by the time I moved on from there I had earned my projects management wings, acting as the leader of many change programs which (mostly) went according to plan. There were some car crashes of course, but they got fewer, so I must have been getting better! Sometime while there I attended an eye-opening training program and came across some very bright cookies doing organizational development at Roffey Park. My training with these guys made me finally realize that what really goes on in business is a human interaction, and that to get great outcomes in business all you needed was great humans. Then it all started to fall in place. Great business outcomes are about great people, so if all humans are great this should be easy right? Wrong! There's so much that we humans create and fantasize about and are scared of that prevents us from being at our best. I strongly believe that organizations that can remove these blocks and find a proper level of human connection can build trust, and once you have trust then we can really start to go places. I took an MSc in organizational and people development through Roffey Park and in 2012 backed my learning with the establishment of Poppyfish People Development, fulfilling a career dream of helping business capitalize on the potential of the human in the system and engaging in client work across multiple industries and coming across Steve Jarrett and his SPECTRUM model in 2013. As opposites attract we make a good team.

Coming Together

We met when a mutual friend and client, Ian Cresswell, a people-focused leader to whom we are both indebted, intuitively thought we would work well together in his organization. We did. Nick is more cautious and careful, methodical, analytical, and checks everything, and Stephen dives in, cracks on, and says, "Everything will be alright in the end, if it is not alright it is not the end!" (Indian Proverb). Stephen thinks getting stuck in is the answer and Nick knows that to reflect and think about it first often gets a better outcome. Nick acts as the brake to Stephen's accelerator pedal and on average we work off each other well. Like many relationships the only challenges come when we both want to steer. We both believe in the power of dreams and that positivity and energy really count for something.

Our work together has been varied, challenging, but always rewarding, working as coaches, consultants, trainers, facilitators, and leaders of learning and behavior change for many individuals, teams, and businesses. In a nutshell, we help our clients align people performance with organization performance. We do this in many different industry sectors, including technical services, information technology, scientific research, start-ups, and construction. We don't spend much on marketing; instead, our growth has been through word of mouth and personal recommendation. We think that is important. It's part of our own brand.

We are guided by the simple principle that the best people build the best businesses. In a world increasingly driven by technical development and big data, workplaces remain a human environment. The performance of your business depends massively upon the talents, motivations, and behaviors of the people that work within it.

We want to see those people at their best, in a space where their talents shine.

To work with us is to recognize that each of us has our own dreams, aspirations, and desires, and that if we can tap into this rich vein of motivation then we can all fly. Our motives for writing this book are to capture some of the "common sense" activities that we think make a difference to how businesses perform. Most of what you will read here is not rocket science, but it is hopefully practical and resonates enough with your own experiences to allow you to feel confident and capable at making great things happen. It's a chance for us to share what we have learnt through the blood, sweat, and tears of our work, and hope that you find the content rewarding.

Blood, Sweat, and Tears

Blood, Sweat, and Tears is a simple to follow trilogy of books, with most of the advice you could need to develop, grow, and succeed as a manger or leader in any team or business from a one-man self-employed person to a large enterprise. The ideas in this book have come about after many years of consulting practice—working with the great, the good (and even the bad). From seeing businesses fail and learning from their mistakes through to businesses that did great things and were successful the authors have picked up the best practices and principles that guide success. This book attempts to share our learning. The principles, ideas, and ways of thinking that are outlined in these pages will help to focus your thinking with regard to self-development, team development, and business development.

According to Bloomberg, 8 out of 10 entrepreneurs who start businesses fail within the first 18 months. A whopping 80 percent crash and burn after having the chance to send out only one lot of corporate Christmas cards. But why? The reasons that businesses fail are painful inasmuch as many of them are easily avoided.

At the surface level the primary reason businesses fail is that they run out of cash. But the reasons for that are deeper than apparent shallowness of the cash drawer. In our combined lives as consultants we have seen plenty, advised many, and been ignored by lots!

How can you avoid these failures? Only through the application of blood, sweat, and tears.

We have created BLOOD, SWEAT, and TEARS as an acronym for all the things that you can do that will help to drive success—setting out attitudes, behaviors, and practices that you can follow to help you achieve your and your company's goals. The ideas are developed throughout the following pages, with each letter of the acronym given its own chapter.

The acronym explained:

Book One

BLOOD is the life source of your success:

B stands for **BRAND**: Can you build the right brand for you and your business and demonstrate alignment between the two?

L stands for **LEADERSHIP**: Do you have the right skills to understand the needs of others and get the best out of yourself and your team?

O stands for **OPPORTUNITIES**: Can you manage the process of generating leads and prospects and take advantages of the opportunities that will grow your business?

O stands for **OUTCOMES**: Are you focusing on the right outcomes to hit your goals? How do you set goals and objectives?

D is for **DECISIONS**: Can you make the right decisions that lead to success?

Book Two

SWEAT are the exercises that you should constantly focus on.

S stands for **STRATEGIC DIRECTION**: Do you have the right vision, mission, strategy, and structure for your business to succeed?

W stands for **WHAT IF?** Do you know what to do in those "What If. . ." moments? Can you and your team be resilient or forward thinking enough to take steps to avoid confusion and chaos in a fast-changing world?

E stands for **EVIDENCE**: Can you find the evidence to back your intuition? What can you do to get the information you need to act for the best?

A stands for **ACTION**: Can you overcome the urge to procrastinate and take action when you need to?

T stands for **TIME:** Can you get your timings right and manage everything you have to do in a way that keeps you in control?

Don't forget "and": don't forget yourself and enjoyment and quality time and family and friends, etc.

Book Three

TEARS are the things that will refresh and reward you.

T stands for **TRAINING**: Are you training the right people in the right way—the essential tool that makes you ready to cope with the demand of tomorrow? Train people all the time and so they can leave—then treat them so they don't want to!

E is for **ENCOURAGEMENT**: To get the best out of others you must know what drives and motivates them. Can you give encouragement to others and know where to find your own?

A stands for **ANNOUNCEMENTS**: DO you announce the important things in the right way? How can you present for maximum impact?

R stands for **REVIEW**: Do you take time to reflect and review the past with an eye on the future? Take time at each step of the way to look back what you have achieved, what you can learn from it, and how this can help you for future planning.

S stands for **SUCCESS**: Can you deliver success for you, your team, and your business? How will you know you are succeeding and what to do next? Taking time to enjoy your successes has a narcotic effect, leaving you wanting more!

Our experience tells us that this is what makes a difference in successful organization. If you get it right the benefits can be stunning. Here's what happens if you get it wrong:

If you cannot identify or build your **BRAND** then you'll be faced with confused customers and staff who don't really know what the business (or you if you are the brand) stands for, you'll have to accept that others will define it for you.

If you do not develop the right **LEADERSHIP** skills, you will create anxiety and frustration for others and increase the propensity for false starts and you will have to accept that people will be frustrated. You will start to lose people, starting with the best ones first.

If you fail to act on **OPPORTUNITIES,** then you can expect finances to take a direct hit. The implications of this are obvious. While this is playing out you will generate anxiety for people who will realize that the writing is on the wall.

If you fail to identify the right **OUTCOMES,** then people do the wrong thing. False starts happen, and people get frustrated and confused. You cannot track progress. Tasks never finish. Morale drops. People leave. And so do customers.

If you struggle with **DECISIONS,** then you can expect people to get frustrated and for confusion to reign. Lack of decision making provokes anxiety and slows your business down.

If you fail to define and communicate a **STRATEGIC DIRECTION,** then chaos abounds. Your business becomes a lawless territory without guidance or a moral compass. People make up their own strategy and resist your efforts to pull them away from that because they do not know any better. You will never have buy in and without buy in you will be in a state of constant confusion. You will also be handing over control to the micro-managers.

If you fail to spot and train yourselves for the **WHAT IF ...** moments, then you will create anxiety as people will not feel equipped to deal with change and you will be left behind by the world. You also risk jeopardizing your business by reducing its resilience to the point where the slightest wave or market tremor could threaten its existence.

If you fail to secure **EVIDENCE** for changes you will cause frustration and run the risk of a number of false starts where you thought you were doing the right thing but, as it turns out, you are not. Oops. More prework and evidence might have helped. You'll also have egg on your face and could have just cost the business lots of money.

If you fail to take **ACTION,** you will condemn your business or project to the scrapheap of time. The road to hell is paved with good intentions, so they say. So, sort out your project plan and make it happen.

If you fail to get your **TIMINGS** right you will create inefficiencies, frustration, and will probably lose money. Tasks will slip. And if you ask people to do what they see as the wrong thing at the wrong time you will encounter resistance. Resistance is not futile, that's why we do it.

If you fail to **TRAIN** your people, then your plans will be sabotaged by people who cannot do what you ask of them and who will not be able to grow themselves at a rate that allows them to deliver any growth to your business. People will be frustrated and will not feel important. Good people will leave while the less able struggle. As the old cliché goes: What if we train our people and they leave? Well, what if we don't train them and they stay?

Failure to **ENCOURAGE** people leads to alienation at work and development and strategic goals not being met. In addition, negativity will seep into the workplace and will be visible to customers. A negative team is a poor performing team. You also run the risk of sabotage, where people dig their heels in to actively prevent and delay progress (yes, it does happen!).

If you fail to **ANNOUNCE** what you are doing, then you risk people putting their own reasons behind your motives. Nobody likes surprises and when people see the action but without knowing the reasons they have no chance to buy in, no chance to support, or even realize what is going on. This creates resistance and can even promote fear as people often fantasize about losing their jobs.

If you fail to **REVIEW** then you are condemning yourself to repeating the same old mistakes again and again. Doing the same thing time after time and expecting a different outcome each time is a first definition of madness.

And if you fail to **SUCCEED** then celebrate small wins (because they will always be there) and keep trying, keep working, and think about which of the other 14 areas you needed to work at.

What about the "And?"

But what about that small conjunctive in the middle? The word "and." The word "and" is the glue that effortlessly ties everything together. It gives the three words meaning. Without the word "and" the three words BLOOD, SWEAT, TEARS appear nothing more than a list. But when we bring in the conjunctive "and" the three suddenly have cumulated impact, allowing the three to come together in a more powerful way. So, the "and" is more than just a word, it actually means something and pulls the concept together.

To this end we have devoted a chapter to the "and." So, what is it? In our view the "and" is the personal strength, power, and dedication that you will bring to your working world when you are at your best. The "and" includes your own metal health and physical well-being, it includes looking after your family and those around you and finding equal space in your life for all things.

So, read on. Challenge your mind to think creatively about how you can embed these ideas into your everyday thinking, thinking that will help you to define your vision and identify your product, price it correctly, take it to market, get business, make a profit, keep your customers wanting more, motivate and inspire your staff, delight your suppliers, reward your stakeholders and your loved ones, and give you a sense of satisfaction and delight in who you are and what you have achieved.

Our Methods

Throughout this book we employ some old techniques tried and tested since the ancient Greeks and developed further by a multitude of respected gurus, psychologists, organizational development theorists, coaches, management consultants, and successful businessmen and women from around the world. But we also give you new ideas and our latest thinking on some blended approaches which we have used and which we know work. We will give you war stories of where things didn't work—and companies got it so wrong—and compare these to where they got it so right and share that best practices with you, giving you the best chance to set up and run your business or team successfully. We will introduce you to some models to help you conceptualize some of the more important areas.

How you use this book is up to you. You can read the book cover to cover in chapter order or jump directly to the area where you need help today and use it as a standalone chapter without the rest of the book holding you! So, if you just want to target specific areas then of course you can.

We hope very much that you enjoy BLOOD, SWEAT, and TEARS and that you can use it to fuel a wonderful success story.

Steve Elkins-Jarrett and Nick Skinner
London
April 2018

CHAPTER 1

An Introduction to Behavior and the SPECTRUM Model

Before we get started with *Blood, Sweat, and Tears* we need to introduce an important concept. Much of this book is about behavior. It is about what you can do to get the best outcomes for you and your business, and how you can do it. "Doing" things involves behavior.

What Is Behavior?

Behavior can be defined as the combination of what you do, what you say, how you say it, and what facial expressions and body language you use in the process. On the basis of these elements, other people make assessments and judgments of you, and you make assessments and judgments about them, both consciously and subconsciously. Our behaviors are complex and open to many influences. Our education, our environment, our role models, our genetic heritage, our situation, our culture, our values, and our society's rules all combine to shape our behavior.

However, behavior is not set in stone. It is a choice. You can choose, and therefore change, what you do, what you say, how you say it, and what facial expressions and body language you use. The ability to choose or adapt your own behavior can generate a major increase in personal effectiveness. The key to development is being aware of, and able to use, the most appropriate behavior for a situation.

Man has studied behavior for thousands of years. The ancient Greeks compared human behavior to earth, water, fire, and air. Freud, Jung, Fromm, Rodgers, and Pavlov have been fascinated by behavior. Psychologists have labeled behavioral types with words. Some of these models are lost to time, like Mar's facial shapes or Pavlov's canine types. Others such as Eric Fromm's work dating back to the 1930s and work that appeared in the second half of the last century, such as Myers–Briggs Type Indicator (MBTI), DISC, and LIFO, are still very popular in the Western world as management tools. The unkind observer would look at our world from the outside and say that all these profiles are pretty similar. And the truth is that, to a point, that observer would be right. The MBTI focuses on four dimensions of personality: our preference for the inner or the outer world, the way we gather information, the way we make decisions, and how we organize and structure our lives. It then combines these to 16 personality types that are extracted. It's a highly technical model that can be challenging to remember. People who have taken it can normally remember what the first letter indicates; E for extrovert or I for introvert, but the other two letters are less well retained. Another common tool also known by its acronym, DISC, focuses on four essential behavioral preferences determined from outgoing or reserved personality traits versus task focus or people focus. From these dimensions the model describes an individual in terms of: Dominant, Inspiring, Supportive, and Cautious. A third model, LIFO, presents a situational assessment of behavior classified into four leadership preferences: Supporting giving (SG), Controlling taking (CT), Conserving holding (CH), and Adapting dealing (AD). These are all excellent models and worthy of use. The problem though with many of these models is that you need to be "qualified" to be permitted to use them, which is costly to administer. Our preferred model of behavior, SPECTRUM, that we refer to throughout this book, is based on colors not words and, we believe, is less expensive, more practical, easier to use and explain, and has the great advantage that it is understandable by all staff at all levels from day one. We've used it with many, many clients with great success, from Board Members to Refuse Operatives with equal impact. You think behavioral models are complicated and confusing, and that maybe you need a degree in Psychology to understand them? Well, SPECTRUM is different. It does not categorize you into introvert or extrovert but rather categorizes you on a continuum or spectrum between the two extremes. It also blends four primary colors of Red, Yellow, Green, and Blue into 18 styles each labeled with a color suggesting the mix of colors used. No one else does this.

The SPECTRUM Model

SPECTRUM is a behavioral model designed to help us understand more about an individual's behavior. Organizations and teams, as aggregates of individuals, therefore can be said to exhibit their own behavioral norms and preferences, which gives an indication of culture.

The SPECTRUM evaluation[1] uses a simple system of colors to explain our different behavioral preferences and tendencies. The four basic colors—RED, GREEN, BLUE, and YELLOW, give us the overview. Your responses to the questionnaire will generate two colors being assigned to you. One color for "normal" behavior and one for "stressed" behavior. The colors are easy to understand:

Think of RED—what do you imagine? Fire, Blood, Heat, Danger. Change these words for assertive, risk taking, hot headed, strong minded, action oriented, and you have a short profile of red behavior.

Think of BLUE and you could be thinking cold, water, sky, icebergs. Substitute these words for calculating, calm, unemotional, logical thinking, and safety and you have blue behaviors.

GREEN might include nature, trees, ecological ideals, peace. Substitute these words for friendly, growing relationships, strong ideals of fairness, and justice and you can understand how someone with a "green" preference may behave.

Lastly, imagine YELLOW and you may see the sun, brightness, and maybe gold. Substitute these words for positive, smile, warm, and happy and you will see the key characteristics of yellow behavior.

The theory here is that if you understand yourself , then you can learn how to tune into others, and for the first time we introduce and ask you to understand and keep in mind this important phrase: "We are taught as children to treat others the way that WE would like to be treated, this is wrong! We have to start treating others as THEY would like to be treated!"

---

[1]Spectrum is outlined in full in the book *Across the Spectrum, What Colour Are You* by Stephen Elkins-Jarrett and available from Business Export Press.

Your SPECTRUM Profile

You can take your own profile easily enough by going online at www .evaluationstore.com and selecting "How effective am I?" Then answer the questions. Your 30-page detailed report will be e-mailed to you as a PDF. It will help you answer the following important questions:

- How Introvert or Extrovert do you think you are?

  Introvert comes from the Latin word "intro" meaning "inward" and vertere meaning "turning." It describes a person who tends to turn inward mentally. *Introverts are energized within themselves* sometimes and as such tend to avoid large groups of people, feeling more energized by time alone.

  An **Extrovert** is a person who enjoys talking to and being with other people. They are energized by being with others. This partly explains why they make great eye contact, because it is a source of energy for them. Extroverts love parties, talking on the phone, and meeting new people.

- How task or people focused are you?

  A task-oriented person is one who focuses on the task or series of tasks at hand, as well as all procedures necessary to achieve the task. This logical person is less concerned with the idea of catering to the needs and wants of others but is likely to be more concerned with finding technical, step-by-step solutions for meeting specific goals. In other words, a task-oriented person might ask, "What steps can we take to meet our quarterly financial goals?"

  A people-focused person understands the importance of placing a tremendous amount of time and focus on meeting the needs of everyone involved in the assignment. They like to collaborate and use emotion rather than logic. They are more likely to ask, "How can we build the kind of employee productivity that brings about success within the company?"

- How do you change in moments of stress?

  In stressful situations our behavior changes. Some people become more aggressive, driven to direct action with more of a fight response. Others go slower, applying a hand brake to their behavior that can frustrate others. Some become more emotional. Others again become flippant and appear to lack focus. Your profile will help you explore your own reaction, identify the actions of others, and understand what you might do to keep the relationship strong.

- What motivates you to make a decision?

  Your color preference might indicate your preferred drivers. Are you driven by the desire to win, to see fair play, or have fun or to follow a sequence in a methodical way to reach your goal irrespective of others? These are red, green, yellow, and blue responses. Are you driven by bonuses, prizes, quality time off? Do you enjoy flexible work with flexible start and finish times? Do you want to be involved? To be asked or told? Being praised and thanked? Never making mistakes? By the book? Compliant? Accurate? Complete? Your profile will teach you more about yourself and how to work with others.

Behavior is simply the words you use (content) together with a pitch, tone, and volume. The eye contact you use, the facial mask you pull, and the body language you show all combine together to get your message across. We all "catch" this from others, judge it, assess it in milliseconds, decide what the other person really means, and then respond using our own behaviors back. The trick is to be able to read others quickly and then treat them how they want to be treated. The SPECTRUM model gives us a simple tool to manage and understand this complex phenomenon. We can use the colors to help read others and to help us determine what we need to do. As a model it is a "simplification of reality" and yet our practical experience is that this stuff works.

Let's Look at How You Might Use This

If I work for someone with a predominantly red profile, then what does that person expect of me? The chances are he wants me to be quick to act, responsive to his demands, and to be a confident self-starter using my initiative to carry out tasks as he would. Speed matters.

Mr Blue on the other hand wants me to be thorough, careful, analytical, check twice before handing over as complete error free and fit for purpose. Doing things the right way is important.

The upbeat Mrs. Yellow wants me to have a social relationship with her, enjoy my work, laugh and share a sense of humor, be a team player, and above all make her look good at all times—let her take the credit. Creativity is important.

Finally we see Miss Green. She wants perfection, sets and expects a high standard and for you to always do your best, try hard and do the right things. With her the truth, justice, honesty, and integrity will be rewarded. It is very important to her that you are OK. This person is kind and helpful and will ask and coach you and ask for support back. Collaboration is important.

Understanding SPECTRUM
Your simple guide to understanding behaviour

RED
Task focused extroverts
Extroverts who want to win, compete, get things done, finished, completed quickly and efficiently, money is important as is status and being in charge of all relationships and things.

EXTROVERT

YELLOW
People focused extroverts
Extroverts who want to be liked and at the centre of everything, funny, witty, charming and popular, gadgets, technology and teamwork are important, so is being involved.

TASK FOCUS

PEOPLE FOCUS

BLUE
Task focused introverts
Introverts who want to get things done by the book, rules, traditions, compliance, health and safety first, error free, double checking, organisation and systems are important.

INTROVERT

GREEN
People focused introverts
Introverts who want to be valued and appreciated without asking, thanked and rewarded with praise, sets high standards for self and others, trusted, loyal, helpful, kind and justice and truth are vital.

These base colors of Red, Yellow, Green, and Blue tell us something, and it makes lots of sense to keep our understanding at this top level. The full SPECTRUM model includes blends of colors where preferences overlap. Thus, we get 18 colors. These give the subtle nuances that make you the individual that you are today. Most of us have a dominant behavior color that is supported by other colors that are less dominant, meaning that mixed profile colors such as magenta, emerald, or tan are common. In practice, we find clusters in organizations. For instance, technical roles where application of process and procedure are important tend to be the space where blues, aqua, and maroons tend to congregate. This is not surprising as the job plays to their behavioral strengths. Creative industries on the other hand tend to show greater yellow characteristics and less blue behavior. It's just the way we like our organizations to be. As humans, it's how we shape our workplaces. It's driven by culture and the needs of the job.

In this book we draw on the SPECTRUM model to help us explore the actions that you might like to take. Each color has its own strengths and weaknesses. Anybody can be one color all the time, but if you are, then the chances are you will not be very effective. Some situations call for red behavior; think of times when you need to be dynamic, fast, outcome driven, and competitive. Some situations call for blue behavior; requiring a methodical focus and attention to detail and process. Some situations require yellow behavior; the demonstration of confidence, infectious optimism and creativity. And some require green behavior when we need to be caring, supporting, and with a focus on the other person.

We have found this model to be highly effective, practical and memorable. After just a short exposure to the model people are able to apply it in the real world to look at others. Some colors are easy to see in others. For instance, Donald Trump probably has an orange profile—an extrovert, confident, fast, energetic, competitive, and tries to be a winner. Consistent with high yellow, his love of Twitter as a communication tool shows a preference for new methods of communication that utilize new technology. You can expect people with an orange profile to be early adopters of new technologies because they are keen supporters of new gadgets and change. His predecessor, Obama, with his apparently softer, personal and more collaborative style was probably greener in his behavioral preferences.

Certainly, many of the more famous introverts, such as Mahatma
Gandhi, Bill Gates, and Mother Teresa, show many more characteristics
of blue, green, and aqua. Looking at their behavior in this way is helpful.
Once you know another person's color you can then simply mirror them
and match their demands with your performance. If you want to succeed
and build strong connections with Donald Trump, then you will probably
need to show drive, ambition, assertiveness, and a direct approach with
pace, all of which are characteristics of high red or orange behavior and
likely to be seen by him as positive behaviors. Using the same behaviors
to build bonds with Barack Obama or Bill Gates is less likely to succeed.
Instead, they would probably be more willing to warm to a more personal, collaborative, detailed, and measured approach.

I Haven't Taken the SPECTRUM Profile, Does That Matter?

In a word, No. While having your own profile makes all kinds of sense
and will help you make the personal connection with much of our content, it is by no means compulsory. By now you will have already picked
up enough of an awareness off the model to think how it may be applied
and how you might make use of it. This awareness and understanding
will hold you in good stead as you work through the ideas in this book.
SPECTRUM is a model of behavior, and models are used to make sense
of the world. You are free to use it—in fact you are now qualified in the
use of it—and we hope that whether you have your own profile to hand
or not, the content that follows will be equally applicable and helpful.

The crux of the matter comes down to this: If you can read a situation,
understand the needs of others, and amend your behavior accordingly,
then you are showing great signs of emotional intelligence, and these will
support your quest to be a successful business leader.

CHAPTER 2

B Is for Brand

Can You Build the Right Brand for You and Your Business?

"Your brand is what people say about you when you are not in the room!"
—Jeff Bezos

A brand is a unique design, sign, symbol, words, or a combination of these, employed in creating an image that identifies a product, service, or even an individual and differentiates it from its competitors.

Branding creates your desired perception and positioning within your market and allows people to differentiate you from your competition. It improves the recognition of your service or product, inspires others by the messages it sends, and allows focused marketing around a theme. In doing this it can drive decision making (for you, your team, and your customers) and build trust and loyalty around your product. All of this ultimately allows you to build value, maximizing the return on your investment and allowing your business to thrive. All these combine to one basic end: they make the customer buy from you!

Having a clearly defined and well-communicated brand enables your customers and clients to remember you. It gives you a chance to emphasize your unique selling point (USP) and tell some of the story behind the brand. It's a chance to celebrate the uniqueness of who you are. For personal branding (i.e., you as opposed to your product or business) it is your chance to be remembered for the right reasons, giving your clients and customers something to rave about. Your brand needs to be authentic. It must be true to your core values which you must demonstrate in everything you say and everything you do. Thus, branding decisions and strategy should have a strong behavioral content. In general, your brand should provide a happy and positive experience for your clients and customers. Creating a brand defines a sense of purpose that your customers sign up to, and if you get this right they will become your evangelists, spreading the good word about your brand and acting as great advertisements for your products. Recommendations become a way of life and you become the first name on any tender list.

Here's a few things to think about when it comes to building your brand.

Branding Improves Recognition

Your brand signals who you are and what you stand for. It does this quickly and with power. For businesses, this aspect of branding is most strongly captured by the logo. This is the general impression of you or your business held by real or potential customers. When creating an image of your products or service provided by your company it is important that it is a real and true reflection of your image. When the logo is seen we instantly know what to expect. It's a great example of just how an image can speak a thousand words. Brand association is the things, words, people, and places that the customer associates with the brand. Think of Disney Corporation and what comes to mind: It's American, cartoons, family focused, magic, Disney World and Disney Land, princesses, castles, Mickey Mouse, and so on. The Brand awareness of Disney is probably the biggest in the world along with Microsoft, Apple, McDonalds, and Coca Cola. But to what extent are people aware of your brand—really?

We attach identities, meaning, and emotional value to logos and symbols, whether we are talking about Mickey Mouse's ears, the enticing golden arches of McDonalds, the swoosh of Nike, or the Union Jack flag of the United Kingdom. Yes, the Union Jack is an iconic brand symbol: see the Union Jack and people instantly associate images of the Queen, red double-decker buses, black taxi cabs, and James Bond. Associating your brand with other mega-brands can reap dividends. Many UK businesses for instance build their products on the back of "brand Britain" in their own campaigning. Turn your mind back to the opening sequence of the London Olympics in 2012, where viewers around the globe watched as James Bond and the Queen skydived out of a helicopter to get the games underway. Well, perhaps it wasn't the real Queen, but you get my point.

Your logo sits at the center of your brand awareness, signaling important messages about quality, loyalty, and even your mission and vision. And color matters. We are huge advocates of the SPECTRUM model of behavior from www.evaluationstore.com. The model, which as a product is young in comparison to many behavioral models, is based on the psychology of the ages, and deploys classic Jungian methods into a simple to understand modern and valid model.

As described in the previous chapter, the model profile is based around two scales. One, is the classic introvert–extrovert assessment. The other, is the task-focused–people-focused approach. The model uses color to understand behavior, and this is important because the colors used can be applied to our review of branding as having the same symbolic content. The main four colors of the SPECTRUM tool are red, yellow, green, and blue. Task-focused extroverts are red; direct, assertive, confident action-oriented people with a "get it done" approach. Yellow keeps the extroversion but instead talks about a people-focused approach, which is about fun, positivity, creativity, and energy. Blue and green are the introverted equivalents of red and yellow. Blue symbolizes low risk, methodical, planning, and detail-focused introverts, while green suggests a high emphasis on quality, empathy, and pleasing others.

Applying this thinking to branding makes absolute sense. Think of businesses you know that have red in their branding. They tend to be direct, get it done business with an emphasis on action and speed. Think Nike, Coke, Virgin, KFC, etc. Yellow logos are more suggestive of creative businesses where fun is important. Blue logos tend to suggest affordable, practical, safe, and risk free. Green logos tend to suggest quality and care (especially these days for the environment). These are often associated with high-end products. Think of Harrods, John Lewis Partnership, Land Rover, Jaguar.

Combinations also work. Tesco combines the directness of red with the dependable practicality of blue. As does Domino's Pizza (and the Union Jack and Stars and Stripes). The thing is that while there are exceptions our experience tells us that the colors can help say something about your brand. The right colors fit in a way that just makes sense. If they are wrong, well, it just doesn't feel right. Would the red and blue of London Underground work as well if it were yellow? Probably not. Getting the color right is important.

You can change this of course. McDonalds, famous for their red livery and "golden arches," fits this model nicely. With a brand emphasis on speed and fun that was reinforced by the appearance of the clown Ronald McDonald, the business created a brand that we all recognize. More recently, McDonalds has seen a shift in its brand definition, and now you see greener behaviors in their establishments and packaging. What does green stand for? Quality, ethical, caring, and healthy. You can see the shift in McDonalds in terms of their brand and in their behavior, where they are now keen to support the healthy aspects of their menu and to reinforce their corporate ethical values.

When it comes to branding an individual of course you won't have a logo, but you will have a way that you want to appear to your clients, and this way of dressing, looking, or behaving becomes part of your brand. Think of famous celebrities who have defined a carefully controlled style or brand in the way that they look. Male comedians are a good place to look for this. There tends to be a couple of distinctive types. One is the suited and smart looking comedian. You know the guy, he's always wearing a sharp suit with shiny shoes, or perhaps an open collared shirt with a jacket. He often commands the stage with a confident style that adds to his authority. And you always see him in that outfit, whether he is on stage doing his act or appearing on a late-night chat show. His suit is part of his brand. He presents it to you all the time. Think Michael McIntyre, Jack Dee, and Jimmy Carr. The other type of comedian is the scruffy looking local lad, normally with a more direct style (and often more adult in terms of his material). He too presents a consistent image, making him and his product instantly recognizable. You never see him in a suit, it just would not fit with his brand. Think Mickey Flanagan or Milton Jones.

As an individual you need to think what message you want to send out. A consultant who turns up in a client's premises in a sharp suit one day and jeans and t-shirt the next would be sending out mixed messages. I know consultants who drive a red sports car and write with a $400 fountain pen just because it is what they think the client expects. It's all part of personal branding. Personal branding is more about what you will *never* see them do rather than what you would expect to *always* see them do! In the example above, the consultant would never use a Bic Biro, or use a 900 cc hire car when his sports car is being serviced, or dress in a $80 cheap suit, or wear $20 shoes from a high street shop. But he might arrive in a bigger bolder car, add a Hugo Boss to his suit collection, wear Gucci snake skin shoes, and use a new 24C gold Aspinal pen.

Branding Builds Value

If you want to see the value of a large business what would you do? Quite likely you'd take a look on the Stock Exchange to get a share value that would allow you to determine a value for the business. What you will notice is that for most companies at least the businesses listed are valued at many times the actual asset value of the company. Much of this upgrade is due to branding, giving the company a power and weight in its market over and above the actual value of its component parts. A strong brand usually guarantees future business.

Having a strong brand can also allow you to charge more than your competitors for a product or service. People believe they are getting more than just the raw product. Marks & Spencer in the UK built a brand based around high quality and value with adverts for products with taglines like "These aren't just potatoes, these are M&S potatoes." And of course, those items can be sold for a higher price. Building a brand builds value. It has meaning and that meaning can be translated into hard cash. And it is associated with brand quality, the perception of the quality of the experience or product or service that the customer has received and is often described as how well and how much you got for your money. So, in a hotel you would expect a clean, comfortable room with a good food and drink service that was priced to my expectations. Disney's is a commitment to producing an unparalleled entertainment experience, based on its legacy of quality creative content and exceptional storytelling. And most critically, as a consumer I am willing to pay extra for that.

Brands also build ethical value. Most significantly, your decisions around branding send a message about your values. The image conveyed in the brand must be in keeping with the values of the business. Your brand presents your values, demonstrating to the customer what it is that you stand for. It will draw them to you.

Branding Inspires Others

Having a brand gives those around you a clear signal of what you believe in and gives them a chance to fall in step with you. If their values are aligned with your brand values then people will be prepared to work harder, longer, and faster because they believe in what the brand stands for. For individual branding or for small businesses this has a direct correlation with personal leadership, as we will see in the following chapter. But in larger businesses, your brand becomes a rallying point, and can even be the reason why people want to work for you. The brand can build the culture. It's a powerful thing.

Branding can also be used for employee motivation within teams, when much of the same psychology comes into play. Revising and relaunching a brand identity for your team can reengage people and allow them to fully engage with the business. Most businesses will revise and update their brand messages every so often, and in our experience when this happens it does reinvigorate teams within the business who have a chance to redirect and refresh what it is that they do. If you head up a team or department, think about what brand you are creating. Do you demonstrate behavior in keeping with the overall brand? Think too about creating a specific brand for your business, perhaps supported by your own mission and vision statement, and even possibly a team charter of behavior. Think about what your team does. What feeling or flavor does it leave in the minds and hearts of people in the other teams that your team or department interacts with? What signals do you send and what do you do to generate trust and enable you to build value? Realigning your team behind a rebranding can inspire your own people and those in the teams around you.

Branding Drives Decision Making

Because your brand defines or sets down a clear expectation of what you stand for, it actually serves to simplify decision making. Decisions will be looked at in a later chapter of this book, but a clear brand can have a strong impact in how decisions are made. Because a brand is so closely aligned to vision, it signals a beacon that all decisions can relate to. Faced with a choice of decisions, all I need to do is compare each option against our brand to see which decision is the most consistent with that brand and its values. This is extremely important in big businesses, where individuals making the decision might be far removed from the people setting the vision and driving the brand. For small businesses and individuals, branding and value are so closely aligned as to be almost indistinguishable. If a brand and value are in conflict, cognitive dissonance will arise, where the two seems to be at odds with each other. This will probably lead to confusion in the minds of the individual and definitely will do so in the minds of the client.

Branding Focuses Marketing

Your marketing and advertising will be built around your brand. As before, your style and values will help you to define the way you choose to promote and market your product or service. This also works by ensuring your focus is neither too broad nor too narrow. Your brand should mean something to your target audience. Along with your logo your brand might well be reinforced with a slogan or strapline. This is simply a few words or catchy phrase that sends a clear message of your brand and values and which can be remembered and quoted by your customers again and again—like "never knowingly undersold"—John Lewis. Creating one is fun (and often cringeworthy at the same time). The best are short and to the point.

Consider: and think about these and what they say to you:

Like sleeping on a cloud (Sealy)

Milk from contented cows (Carnation)

Save Money, Live Better (Wal-Mart)

I'm lovin' it (McDonalds)

When you care enough to send the very best (Hallmark)

Just Do It (Nike)

Finger Lickin' Good (KFC)

Have it your way (Burger King)

And Disneyland's "the happiest place on earth"

Branding Creates Trust

In June 2013 philosopher Onora O'Neill delivered an excellent TED talk on trust, with the message that if you want to build more trust you must show yourself to be trustworthy. The talk was delivered at the British Houses of Parliament, amidst politicians whose reputation of trust has, in recent years, not been the best. Politics as a "brand" has suffered as a result. But building trust is a big part of branding. By building and presenting a brand you are giving your customers a chance to buy into you and to trust you. You are giving them not just the product or service, but all the "extra" aspects that come as part of the brand. Take Walt Disney's vision, which is to be the preeminent leader in the field of family entertainment. Its mission is to be one of the world's leading producers and providers of entertainment and information, which excels in being a diversified international family entertainment and media company. Families are based around trust. The brand must symbolize that trust. Disney has excelled at this and in so doing has created lifelong brand loyalty that starts from an early age. Many of us buy in to the brand without question. Most adults will have childhood memories of Disney and they tell these to their children and grandchildren. It provides a warming legacy of feel good that families can sign up to. It's a way of living your family dreams. That's what you're looking for in your brand.

Much of this is intangible. But by presenting customers and clients with a clear brand you are also giving them something that they understand, can sign up, and, most importantly, trust. If you demonstrate a brand that is professional, caring, thorough, and honorable then people will be attracted to you. Purely and simply, if your brand does not portray trust then you are on to a loser. End of story.

All of these points are as true for individuals as they are for businesses. As an individual your brand is the feeling that you leave in the minds and bodies of others after you have left the room. How do you want people to feel after having met you? Is it important that you are seen to be happy or serious? Task focused, or people focused? A good listener or a good talker?

You can learn from the big brands here and think about what it is that they are trying to create and how they do it.

Also, remember that if you do not create your own brand then others will do it for you. This will be based on all the experiences of you and your services, good and bad, and will be influenced by their own thinking. Much better to create and communicate your own, proactively. Have you ever tried "Googling" yourself? That is, search for yourself on Google to see what comes up. It is what others are doing and it matters.

We worked with a client once who wanted to present an image to the world of being a people-focused company, yet if you Googled them one of the first hits that was returned was a story about blacklisting of individuals. It makes life very difficult when you say one thing and yet people see evidence of the opposite! It creates doubt in the mind of the observer. The hard thing is that it is very hard to divorce what you say from what you do. Words and actions are both powerful when on their own, but when you get the chance to see words and actions alongside each other, what do you believe? Yes, you've got it, the actions always win out.

Here's a nice example of that. Imagine you are walking along a road with a letter intended for a house some way along the street. It's a nice day and you are feeling good about yourself. The sun is shining, there are a few kids riding their bikes, and a dog is barking. It sounds pretty angry. As you get closer to your neighbor's house the barking gets louder, and you realize that the noise is actually coming from a dog in your neighbor's yard. The house itself looks lovely, like something taken straight from a picture postcard. As you approach the garden gate on the approach to the house you stop momentarily. There, on the other side of the pretty little wooden gate, is the dog. It's a big and mean Rottweiler, mad looking and barking in a frenzy. Its eyes are wild, its mouth is frothing, and it is straining at the rope that is tied to the wall next to the porch. Luckily the rope is not as long as the garden path, so instead of ripping your throat out the dog stands, strained, staring at you with mad eyes. Its intent is clear. Open that gate at your peril. Now, you've got an errand to run, a letter to post, but right now that doesn't seem like the way that you want to be spending your time. Much more sensible maybe to turn away and either try again another time, or maybe catch your neighbor next time you see him on the street. Looking again at the dog you see a sign around its neck. The sign reads "I'm friendly, I don't bite."

You are now in a dilemma. You see the words, but the actions of the dog don't make sense when compared against them. You're confused. What if the words are right and the dog doesn't bite? Well, that sure doesn't look like a friendly dog. The rational part of your brain is maybe saying to you; "Hey, you can trust the sign, those words have been put there and they must be true." But at the same time another part of your brain, undoubtedly led by the amygdala, that little central part way down deep in your brain that controls all your gut instincts and animal reactions, says to you "No way, don't go in there, he'll rip your throat out." The rational study of the words rarely wins against that human instinct and feeling.

What would you do?

Few of us would believe the words. Most of us would believe what we see. Most of us would choose to ignore the sign because the evidence of the actions really does speak louder than the words. It's not just a cliché. And this is exactly as it is in the workplace. Espoused culture—that which we say and want others to believe—is one thing, but what we actually do and what others actually experience is another. The impact on your personal brand is significant.

We've all encountered the boss who says, "my door is always open" but with whom you can never get past his officious PA yet alone make an appointment. The actions and the words do not match. Think carefully about your brand, for others will hoist you by it. To build your own brand you must start deep within yourself.

At the heart of your brand sits your values. These influence the very way that you behave. They sit at the heart of your personality and influence everything that you do. Some people's values are easy to see. For some others it can be harder. Some people wear their values hard on the outside for all to see, and often it shows in their career and family choices that they make. Religious ministers, for instance, often demonstrate openly a very clear connection between their values and their career option. The outward signs of their values, such as the way they dress, the objects they wear, and the words they say are all hopefully in alignment. Their brand is clear to see. But for your own self this might be a less straightforward connection. Your own values might not show so strongly on the outside but look inside yourself and they will be there.

How to Identify the Values of Others

There is a simple test here and it's to do with followership. In general, people are prepared to go along with you all the while their values are not compromised or threatened. But cross the line and you will very quickly see that person push back. Imagine a group of kids walking down the street, their minds set on a bit of fun, or what my grandad would have called "high jinks." A little light-hearted running and shouting is ok, they might even knock on a few doors and run off before the householder answers the door, but when the gang leader suggests that they smash the windows on the phone box at the end of the street the other members of the gang may falter. Some, whose values are not threatened, may go along with it anyway. Others will feel much more uneasy, leading to a drop in energy for the gang's activities and possibly even a termination of the friendship by breaking away and heading home. I know what I would have done, and in fact I did, when I really was in that situation at some point in my youth. Stepping over the line from fun to vandalism was a values line that I wasn't prepared to cross. The purpose of the story is to demonstrate that it is easier to identify a person's values when you ask them to betray them or do something they are uncomfortable with. And so it is at work. People will behave in a way that is consistent with the values, but when values are stretched they become disengaged or will leave.

How to Identify Your Own Values

It is almost impossible to successfully brand a business around a theme that you do not believe in. If your own values, beliefs, and behaviors do not represent the values, beliefs, and behaviors of the business then customers will be confused and will not buy from you. So, to create your business brand you must first understand your own values. Knowing these values will identify your passions, and these are the things that you will hold dear and will put most energy into. One very helpful way of identifying your own values is a rather macabre exercise. Simply ask yourself what would you like others to say about you after you have died? Take some time to sit quietly and write your own eulogy, a speech to be delivered by another person in the event of your death. What do you want to be able to say about yourself?

Consider the following examples:

Firstly, let's consider Ted. Ted is thinking of setting up a business as a debt collector. He has long wanted to work with money and enjoys helping people out. He completes the eulogy exercise and writes this about himself:

> Ted was a family focussed man who always had time for others. His helpful nature and sympathetic approach to life made him an ever-welcome guest in the homes of all that he knew. He showed compassion, was kind and thoughtful to the needs of others. He was a fair man who valued people. He would never let others suffer or be without.

Does that sound like the profile of a debt collector? Maybe not.

Now let's think about Selima. Selima too wants to start a business as a debt collector. Let's see what she had to say about herself:

> Selima was a driven person who relished a challenge. She was firm and uncompromising with a challenging nature that created an

impact with all who knew her. She was fair judge and an expert negotiator. Winning was everything, for there were no prizes in coming second in life. It was her way, or the highway.

Looking from the outside it would appear that Selima might have the personal values that would help her succeed in her chosen career. It's not that Ted could not, of course, but most probably it is Selima that would have the greatest affinity to the role. Her values seem more closely linked to those needed for the role and the personal brand needed to present to the world. Compassionate accommodating Ted might be giving off the message that he is something of a pushover when it comes to debt sob stories. Few people would take that risk with Selima.

Branding your business matters. Your brand allows customers to make an emotional connection to your product or service, allowing your customers and clients to show others that they share important values and beliefs. This leads to higher sales and better brand differentiation. It also leads to loyalty, advocacy, and can even allow you to charge a premium price as customers and clients that show that connection will be more likely to pay a premium for it.

Take a look at the illustration showing the story of a coffee in Paris and you can start to see the effect of branding on price and value. At the bottom left of the graph we see the raw material. Think about a coffee bean grower—he or she works 365 days a year and with staff working at 24/7 to grow coffee beans. It is hard work, labor intensive, and at $3.75 a kilo (2017 prices) this pulls in a good year 10 percent profit and prays for great weather too which can ruin a harvest. Let's say this supplier makes 37.5 cents a kilo.

A coffee producer will buy and process these beans, stick them in a jar, freeze-dry, and sell the same for $25 a kilo—a 667 percent mark up (gross). Profits in Nestle were a small $6.4 million just on Nescafe coffee in the UK (2015) down on the year before but still a sizable profit.

Next in a motorway services coffee shop I put one teaspoonful of a similar product costing a similar amount into a plastic cup, add some milk frothy and a lid, and charge about $3 for it. Costa made $154 million in 2015 in the UK alone. Now I go to a nice restaurant and enjoy a tasty meal to celebrate my birthday, finishing my meal off with a nice coffee, which costs me about $5. I don't mind this, I know it's more than I could pay in Costa on the way home, and I know that I could save myself $5 if I went home and had a coffee from a jar in my own kitchen, but I like the restaurant and I'm prepared to pay more for the ambience and the feeling of being in the place. I'm paying for the brand.

But what if that restaurant was on the Champs-Élysées in Paris, center of fashion and very much part of the "brand France." Now you can have two cups of coffee but pay d two $30 to sit there. You don't mind this because what you are getting is the EXPERIENCE.

If you can sell the experience and not the product, then people will always be prepared to pay more.

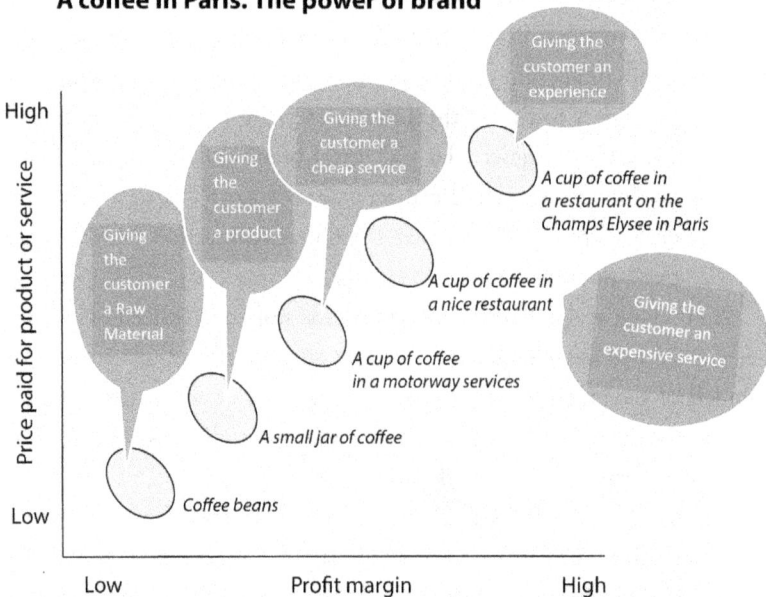

A coffee in Paris. The power of brand

What can you do with your business to give your customers more of an experience?

Branding Your Business

Firstly, take your time, check out others, and make a list of what the services you provide, the technology you use, how well you do this, the people involved in your business, and maybe your community and supply chain and your customers and clients. Look around you at other brands and what they mean to you. How do you feel when you see Ronald McDonald? The Nike Swoosh logo? Or think of Apple, undoubtedly one of the top performing businesses of the modern age. How would you describe their branding?

Think ahead. Projecting your mind into the future is a powerful tool and one that we have often used with good success for clients. What will the world be like then? What will it need? What do you want to be doing? What will your success look like? These are all valid questions to help you shape a view of the future and your place in it. Five years is not a long time (if you doubt me, just throw your mind back 5 years and see where that takes you. The chances are that it will feel like yesterday). Projecting forward is a good way to bypass the obstacles of today and to experience what a future state might look like. What will the market for your business be like in that time frame? How will the world of work have shifted? What will you need from your job? Where will you be in terms of your family and wider commitments? How old will your children be and how will that affect the blood, sweat, and tears that you are able to put into your business?

The best brands are simple and clear, so you need to use simple language to get to a clear proposition. To build your brand start by talking about your business as if you were describing it to a 5-year-old. Be sure to remove all corporate jargon. Then, ask yourself who is your target customer and why would they use you?

You are now starting to define a sense of purpose. Now start thinking about your competitors. Why are they better than you? Once you have done this turn that thinking on its head and say why you are better than them. This will define your USPs that sit at the heart of what you do and that distinguish you from the competition.

The next step is to find yourself a logo or imagery that represents your offering. Consult media for images and metaphors that represent what it is that you want others to experience or feel. For instance, in our work as learning and development consultants we often use imagery around liberation and flying as feelings of freedom, empowerment, and the sense of flying that comes with being at your best. Grab a good range of recent magazines (travel, music, home, professional, food, photography, sport, etc.) or sign up to an online image bank (just search royalty-free images in

Google to unlock a whole world of images). Of course, you could also consult a local marketing business that could do all this for you, and it's always great to have professional input but it is fun to do it yourself and it is of course a lot less expensive. Think about the color of the image. Relate that back to the SPECTRUM model and be sure your color fits your message.

With some imagery in the bag you can start to think about how you want to speak with customers. The language, vocabulary, and style that you use should be consistent with your brand. Do you want to be funky, factual, direct, or instance? People often want to be funny but take this word of advice: if you are not naturally funny then avoid using humor or get input from someone who is. No insult intended, we just want you to avoid those tumbleweed moments. Then sum up how you want your customers to feel in just a few words. You might get to something like:

Impossible is nothing—Adidas.

Reassuringly expensive—Stella Artois.

Because you're worth it—L'Oréal.

The best a man can get—Gillette.

Every little helps—Tesco.

With the short form done you can now add the supporting detail. This need be nothing more than one sentence but one that you can use to support the strapline. An example could be: "We help your nearest and dearest find the peace they need to enjoy their final days."

What kind of business might that be? Yes, even hospices know the power of branding!

Taking time to follow this process, maybe on a piece of paper or—even better—in a facilitated group session with other people's input will help you define your brand. And I don't want to scare you, but you are now having a vision. You are envisaging how you and your business can find a space to thrive and succeed in a future world that is volatile, uncertain, complex, and ambiguous (VUCA). It's a VUCA world, and yet you can see through to a future state. Let this vision of brand inform your thinking and never lose sight of it.

Think about being the best, the fastest, the best quality, the cheapest, the best value for money, the happiest customers, the happiest staff, and so on. If you wind the clock forward 5 to 10 years what is it that you want people to say about your company? Now you are starting to get an idea that can shape your brand.

Remember These Golden Rules about Brand

If you get your BRAND right, you will be able to charge more for your services and earn more profit.

Your BRAND is more than just a logo and a slogan. It has six major benefits but must be built upon your VALUES. If the brand, values, and mission are aligned then they will have more impact and your brand will be more genuine.

COLOR means something when it comes to marketing. Use RED to portray action and speed, YELLOW to show creativity, fun, and a people focus. Use GREEN to emphasize quality and teamwork. Use blue to show facts, logic, and process.

EVERYTHING that you say and do will send others a message about your brand. If you behave consistently with your BRAND, then that message will have more impact.

A great BRAND means something to other people. Not only does it say something about you but by asking them to do business with you they are also making a declaration about themselves.

Make sure your BRAND has something other people can identify with.

CHAPTER 3

L Is for Leadership

Do You Have the Right Leadership Skills to Get the Best from Your Team?

"Management is doing things right; Leadership is doing the right things!"

—Peter Drucker

"Leadership is getting people to follow you anywhere; even if it is out of curiosity!"

—Colin Powell

Leadership is the act of leading a group of people or an organization on a journey, to a destination, to a desired state or through a process of change and having the ability to lead this from the front, by creating, sharing, and inspiring others, to follow them toward the dream and vision. In the field of management science and in organizational development in particular, we often talk about the differences between managers and leaders. Hundreds, and probably millions of books have been written on the topic. Every now and then we come across great little snippets and insights from outside the field that add to the conversation. We will start with one of those from the field of military history, a place to which our reading commonly wanders and where the age-old question of leadership is a theme that is commonly discussed.

The British General William "Bill" Slim was the master of successful military campaigns against the Japanese in the Far East during the

Second World War and the leader of what is often called the "Forgotten 14th" Army, the "forgotten" part coming from the feeling that the folks back home regarded the war in the Far East as a side show compared to the war against Nazi Germany in Europe. The greatest victories of Slim's "Forgotten 14th" were at Imphal, Kohima, and Mandalay, and it was the efforts of Slim's men who secured the liberation of Burma and, combined with the deployment of American might in the Pacific, ensured the defeat of the Japanese Imperial Army. The Burma Star Association says that all in all around one million men fell under the command of the Forgotten 14th, and that it held the longest battle line of any army during the war, reaching from the Bay of Bengal to the borders of China.

Managing and leading an army of that size and across that geographical spread was a monster task. Slim was a General with excellent credentials of success in terms of both strategy and leadership who saw a keen difference between leaders and managers. Slim's comparison runs as follows:

> The leader and the men who follow him represent one of the oldest, most natural and most effective of all human relationships. The manager, and those he manages are a later product, with neither so romantic nor so inspiring a history. Leadership is of the spirit, compounded of personality and vision; its practice is an art. Management is of the mind, more a matter of accurate calculation of statistics, of methods, timetables and routine; its practice is a science. Managers are necessary; leaders are essential.

Slim talks about leadership having a human and personal authenticity gained through the embodiment of personality and vision, against the strict administrative and bureaucratic strengths of the manager.

Leadership is a fascinating area of study and an incredibly important aspect of business. There are many aspects of leadership and we have made a career out of studying it and working with it. In practice it comes down to that one common theme—behavior—for in business as on the battlefield, leadership is little more than what you say and what you do. In this chapter we look at personal leadership; in other words, how to understand and get the best out of yourself for maximum effectiveness and then look at how you can lead (and manage) others. On the way we talk about situational leadership, how teams develop and how team members' individual needs and leadership needs change, and how you can use the SPECTRUM® behavioral model to help you shape your behaviors to show the leadership style that works for you. We will touch on the work of great theories from Blanchard and Hersey, Tuckman, Maslow, and others to illustrate our point and to give some additional concepts to work with.

Personal Leadership

How can you be expected to lead others if you cannot lead yourself? As leader you will set the standard for those around you. In this the top weapon you have in your arsenal is the appropriate use of behavior: Doing the right thing in the right way at the right time. Your own personal leadership style is built on the back of your own personal brand, the formation of which is covered in the previous chapter. As a leader, your actions will build on your brand and will be consistent with it. It is crucially important that what you do has credibility; in other words, it is consistent with your brand and who you are. Great leaders do not fake it. They have a depth of personal passion, commitment, energy, and values that leap from individual to individual with a spark. Their followers know what they believe in and what they stand for. Good leadership sets them aflame. Everything that you say and do develops your personal leadership style. You must be the model of what you want from others and you must be highly self-aware of your moods, your biases, your emotions, and your behaviors—and those of others.

Most crucially, you need to be aware that your positivity will rub off on others. Optimism and a "can do" attitude are contagious. But so are negativity and a "can't do" mind-set. Staying upbeat and showing confidence—especially at times when you actually feel low and lacking in confidence—are basic and important skills for any leader. As they say in the military, never let your men know when you are scared. What you do and how you do it stand for a lot. It influences how your business is perceived and your actions will drive the culture. There is a Vietnamese saying that goes something like this: "The house leaks from the roof down." In other words, what happens in your company is dictated by what goes on at the top. If you are the leader of your company, your department, or your team you must act with 100 percent alignment with everything your company stands for. You must walk the talk and embody the values. For how can you expect others to do this if you do not?

Leading Others

The leadership skills that you need in your business will change as your situation changes, and this is especially true as your team grows. The best leaders are alert to the needs of their team and adjust their style to fit the changing needs of the team. This theory, known as the Situational Leadership Model, was first put forward by Paul Hersey and Ken Blanchard and has achieved worldwide recognition. At the heart of it is a very simply philosophy: the best leaders do the right thing at the right time and in the right way. They know, both instinctively and through experience and learning, when to take a directive approach and tell people what to do, maybe even to the smallest detail. That same manager though will know that, in a different situation, he or she will need to adopt a softer style, allowing the experienced follower or subordinate to find their own best way of performing a task. It might seem like common sense that someone on their first day of work with a new team might need to be treated in a way that is different from the way that an experience team member might need to be treated but, as we will see elsewhere in this book the great thing about common sense is that it isn't that common. Many times, we have walked into an organization to see managers micro-managing highly skilled and highly experienced individuals by telling them exactly what they should do and when to do it while, at the same time, leaving new starters to flounder and find their own way without any support. They couldn't be getting it more wrong, and yet here they are, experienced and professional people, failing miserably to allow their people to perform. On the one hand, the micro-managed experienced staff member feels shocked and controlled at exactly the point in his or her working life when they want to be stepping up and showing they can be independent and set the agenda, while the new member of staff feels lost, scared, and is probably wondering why they ever took the job.

One way we have found of looking at this draws upon the work of Maslow. Abraham Maslow was a sociologist who created a "hierarchy of needs." Developed with a view to studying people in groups, the hierarchy, illustrated, shows the importance of basic physical and safety needs as bedrocks upon which other higher-level needs can be satisfied. For instance, my biological need for air, water, food, and warmth must be satisfied. If they are not, then everything else become meaningless, and I cannot even think about higher-level needs until these basic needs are met. Have you ever tried working in an office that is too cold or too hot? Or in an office filled with people you don't like or feel a connection with? It's impossible to be at your best.

Maslow's Hierarchy of Needs

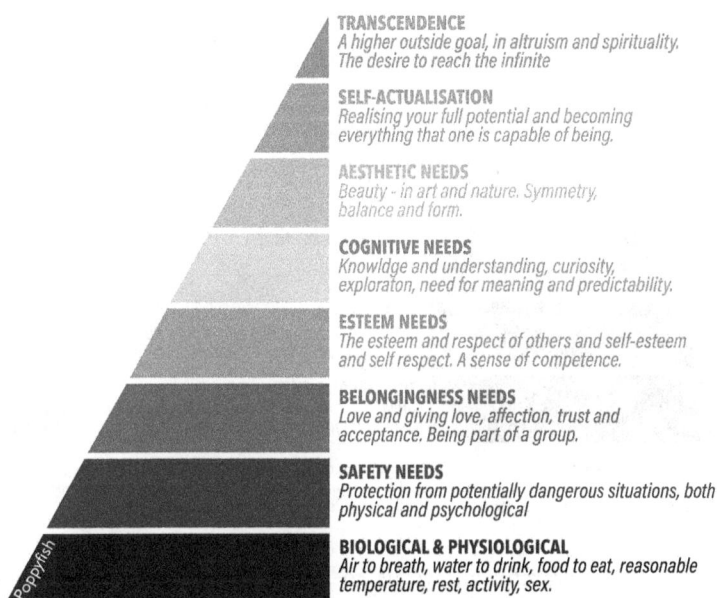

TRANSCENDENCE
A higher outside goal, in altruism and spirituality. The desire to reach the infinite

SELF-ACTUALISATION
Realising your full potential and becoming everything that one is capable of being.

AESTHETIC NEEDS
Beauty - in art and nature. Symmetry, balance and form.

COGNITIVE NEEDS
Knowldge and understanding, curiosity, exploraton, need for meaning and predictability.

ESTEEM NEEDS
The esteem and respect of others and self-esteem and self respect. A sense of competence.

BELONGINGNESS NEEDS
Love and giving love, affection, trust and acceptance. Being part of a group.

SAFETY NEEDS
Protection from potentially dangerous situations, both physical and psychological

BIOLOGICAL & PHYSIOLOGICAL
Air to breath, water to drink, food to eat, reasonable temperature, rest, activity, sex.

Above: An adaptation of Maslow's original work (1943) and later amendments (1954 and 1970). Every person is capable and has the desire to move up the hierarchy toward a level of transcendence. Progress to the next level is dependent on satisfying the levels below it.

We are big fans of Maslow's hierarchy, and we did some work with clients on understanding the importance of the hierarchy for individuals at work, discussing in facilitated group sessions how the hierarchy applied—or did not—to the work of work. What we found is that the hierarchy stood up pretty well to the working environment. This led to the creation of our own development on the hierarchy, which we think represents a basic model of human needs at work. As an employee, if my needs are met at one level then I can move on to the next. However, if my needs are not being met then access to that next level up is denied. When access to a desired level is denied, then I will become agitated and stressed, and will consider my stress responses of fight, flight, or freeze.

Applying Maslow's Hierarchy to the Modern Workplace

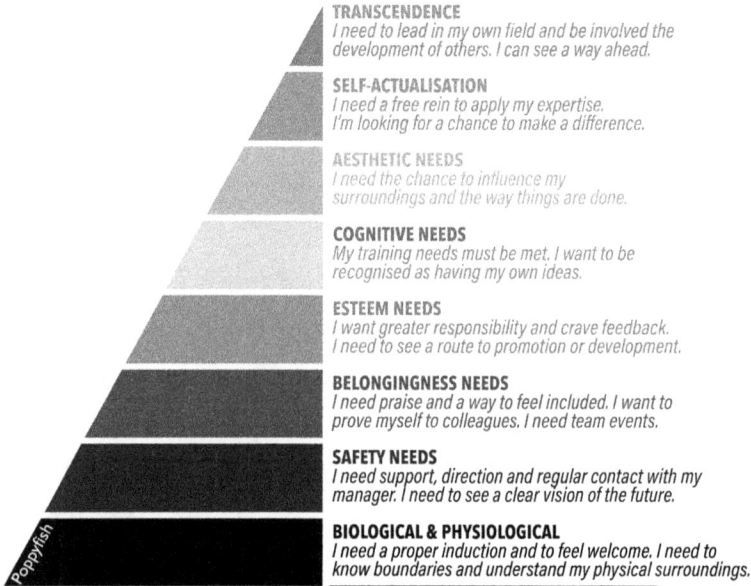

TRANSCENDENCE
I need to lead in my own field and be involved the development of others. I can see a way ahead.

SELF-ACTUALISATION
I need a free rein to apply my expertise. I'm looking for a chance to make a difference.

AESTHETIC NEEDS
I need the chance to influence my surroundings and the way things are done.

COGNITIVE NEEDS
My training needs must be met. I want to be recognised as having my own ideas.

ESTEEM NEEDS
I want greater responsibility and crave feedback. I need to see a route to promotion or development.

BELONGINGNESS NEEDS
I need praise and a way to feel included. I want to prove myself to colleagues. I need team events.

SAFETY NEEDS
I need support, direction and regular contact with my manager. I need to see a clear vision of the future.

BIOLOGICAL & PHYSIOLOGICAL
I need a proper induction and to feel welcome. I need to know boundaries and understand my physical surroundings.

Above: Our own interpretation of Maslow's famous hierarchy, suggesting how our individual needs at work might map against Maslow's 8 hierarchies. If any level is not satisfied this creates discomfort, reduces engagement and prevents the individual moving up to the next level. What level are you at? What level are your team members at? How do you know?

Using the hierarchy allows us to really get to grips with what people need from their leaders. At the entry level I need to have a safe base from which to learn. This means I need a good induction process that allows me to understand what I do and how I am supposed to do it. This also includes some very basic areas such as where I park my car, how far it is to the toilets, is there a canteen, refreshments or food available. This is basic stuff, and once I feel these basic needs are satisfied I can move up to the next level, where my leader needs to step in and give me direction, inspiration, motivation, and feedback. After this I can start to feel included, I want to feel that I am making progress (because I am getting feedback that says so). I have stated goals and objectives that I understand, and I am started to feel part of the team. The dynamic in the team is good, and we enjoy working together and it is good that I can demonstrate my credibility to others. I'm now starting to gain experience and am starting to shape out some ideas around how I'd like my work to develop. I need to be able to see a route to promotion and seek greater responsibility and to feel appreciated. Because of this I crave feedback. This responsibility and focus on the future has allowed me to identify some training needs that I need to be satisfied so that I can be the best person that I can be and so I can take responsibility for taking the team, and me, to the next level. My ideas are important. I now want a way that my ideas can be developed, I need a chance to influence my surroundings. This could be in the way we do things, the processes we use, or even where we sit. By the time I get to this stage my experience is really starting to count. I know that I am worth something to this team, which could not perform as well without me. I'm becoming an expert in my field. Maybe locally, maybe on a wider scale. I don't need to be told what to do, because I have the insight that is gained from experience and I have confidence in my own ideas. I am leading this area, even if my business card doesn't say that I am. My final level is to be recognized as the thought leader that I am, and I need now to show the way to others, to develop them and build them to be the best that they can. This model works. Think about your own team and where they might be on the pyramid. All of this is really useful information to the team leader, who can then use the hierarchy to help understand the needs of the individual. By understanding the needs of the other person we then have a chance of modifying our own behavior to maximize the chances of their needs being met. As I move up the pyramid I am more empowered to lead and it's important that my leader (or manager) allows me that space. You cannot and must not micro-manage above the first couple of levels. As my team moves up the pyramid I can step away and allow them to be great, recognizing that I too am somewhere on the pyramid and that I too have my own needs that must be met. But for managing others the utility of this approach is obvious. If people's needs are being met then they have a great chance of being at their best, and I will have a great team. Easy.

A Maslow of Modern Life ?

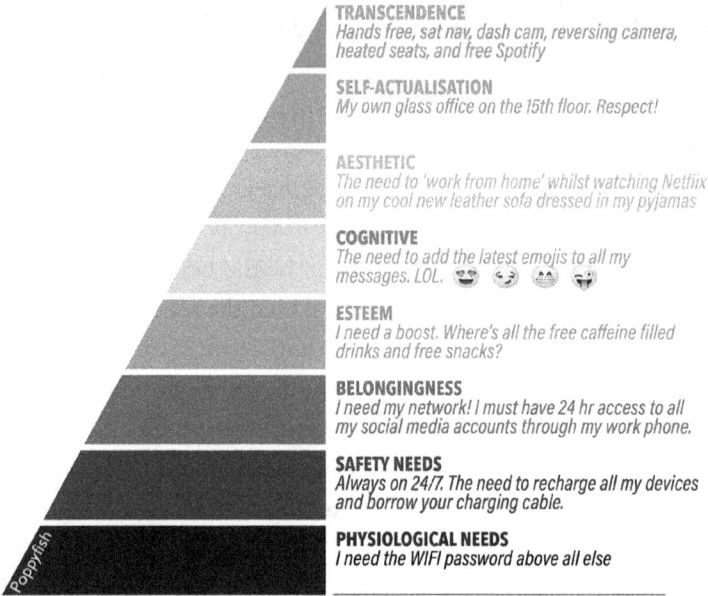

TRANSCENDENCE
Hands free, sat nav, dash cam, reversing camera, heated seats, and free Spotify

SELF-ACTUALISATION
My own glass office on the 15th floor. Respect!

AESTHETIC
The need to 'work from home' whilst watching Netflix on my cool new leather sofa dressed in my pyjamas

COGNITIVE
The need to add the latest emojis to all my messages. LOL.

ESTEEM
I need a boost. Where's all the free caffeine filled drinks and free snacks?

BELONGINGNESS
I need my network! I must have 24 hr access to all my social media accounts through my work phone.

SAFETY NEEDS
Always on 24/7. The need to recharge all my devices and borrow your charging cable.

PHYSIOLOGICAL NEEDS
I need the WIFI password above all else

Poppyfish

Above: No comment needed.

Except it isn't easy. We don't work in isolation. Most work in most businesses is done in teams. Teams are complex and to lead them requires the development of your own emotional intelligence, so you can be aware of the human dynamic of the people you are leading. This requires a people focus that many aspire to but few achieve, especially in moments of stress when we are most likely to become task focused at the expense of all else.

Tuckman Model of Team Development

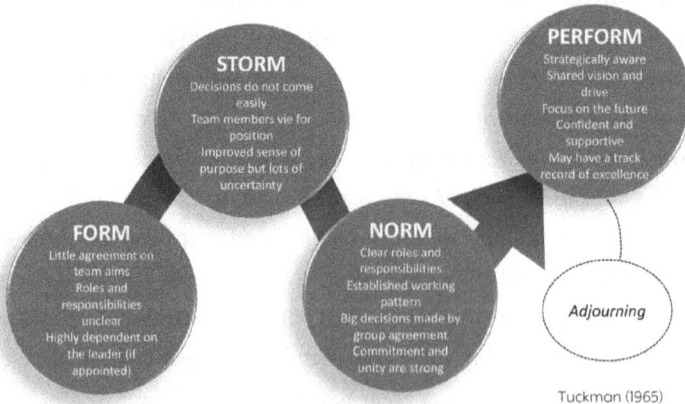

PERFORM
Strategically aware
Shared vision and drive
Focus on the future
Confident and supportive
May have a track record of excellence

STORM
Decisions do not come easily
Team members vie for position
Improved sense of purpose but lots of uncertainty

FORM
Little agreement on team aims
Roles and responsibilities unclear
Highly dependent on the leader (if appointed)

NORM
Clear roles and responsibilities
Established working pattern
Big decisions made by group agreement
Commitment and unity are strong

Adjourning

Tuckman (1965)

Let's introduce the Tuckman Model of Team Development. Bruce Tuckman died in 2013 after having completed a life in psychology and management science, publishing 18 books and more than 100 articles in such areas as motivation, cognition, instructional design, and measurement. He first published his work on team development in 1965; since then it has stood the test of time well. His initial test suggested that teams go through four phases as part of their development. There is no set time that the team spends in each phase, but rather the key aspect is that teams will go through these phases in sequence and, like Maslow, progress to the next level is only possible once certain criteria have been met. Leaders therefore must recognize which phase the team is in and adjust their style accordingly. The model became known as the Form-Storm-Norm-Perform model.

The Form stage covers that time when the team has just formed. In fact, the word team at this stage is not really accurate because what we are talking about is simply a group of individuals. At this stage, immediately on and after formation, there is little shared identity. Lacking self-direction, the group has a high dependence on the appointed leader for guidance and direction. If there is no appointed leader, then there will be a period of disturbance as one emerges. There is little agreement on team aims other than that received from the leader and individual roles and responsibilities are unclear. The leader of this team must be prepared to answer lots of questions about the team's purpose, objectives, and external relationships.

In the Storm stage things are a little more focused, but there is still lots of uncertainty. Decisions don't come easily within the group as team members vie for position as they attempt to establish themselves in relation to other team members and the leader. Clarity of purpose increases but plenty of uncertainties persist. Cliques and factions form and there may be power struggles. This is a hard team to lead, filled with challenges and opinions and often all accompanied with high levels of stress. Working in this kind of team requires high energy and is normally very emotionally charged, so while being in the team can be draining, it is fantastic viewing. There is lots going on and the human dynamic is in full swing. This is the preferred state of teams for TV reality shows, the producers of which use a variety of methods (principally mixing up membership and removing some basic needs) to ensure the team stays in Storm mode.

By the Norm stage things have settled down a little. The leader is now more established, and the team probably has an established way of working on which most of them agree. Agreement and consensus is largely formed among team, where roles and responsibilities are now clear and accepted. Big decisions are made by group agreement, the leader providing input to assist the decision rather than providing pure direction. Smaller decisions may be delegated to individuals or small teams within the group. Commitment and unity is strong. This is a good stage for getting things done. It's calm and focused.

The final stage in the original four-stage model is Perform. Here the team is in a great place to excel. The team is more strategically aware and has a clear sense of purpose and has established standards of performance. The team has a shared vision and is able to stand on its own feet with no interference or participation from the leader. There is a focus on over-achieving goals, and the team makes most of the decisions against criteria agreed with the leader. The team has a high degree of autonomy.

The fifth stage, adjourning, was added by Tuckman at a later date, and makes reference to that phase after the team has been dissolved, when there are still strong feelings toward it. You may inherit a team that has a longing for the halcyon days when they were working together well and effectively, before changes took them away from that. This is a stage where teams tend to be looked at warmly and with a sense of loss. As a leader you just need to recognize the loss and allow people to move on.

Team leaders need to be able to identify where in this model their team is located. What clues can you look for. There are one or two simple ones. Firstly, remember that personnel or physical changes (such as relocation) will instantly put the team into Storm mode. The rapid coming or going of staff means that the team never gets the chance to get to Norm because the human dynamic is always changing. This is especially true in small teams where the impact is greater. But it can also be seen in larger teams. A few years ago, we did some work for a large UK PLC who operated their business in a series of divisions. One of these in particular was giving some cause for concern. The leader of the unit, a senior manager who had been in place for many years, had just stepped down and a member of the wider parent managing body was moved in to take over. He saw a team with high turnover of people where lots of teams seemed to lack direction and had confused priorities. The atmosphere was high energy and the workloads were exhausting. When he spoke to people in the teams they spoke of conflicting demands, no consistency, and a general dissonance between what they thought they were there to do and what they were actually being asked to do. The focus of each subteam was firmly on its own processes, to the effect that silo thinking was the order of the day and work either fell into the chasm between teams or was hurled from one team to the next like a hand grenade. Customers were unhappy and relied on a small network of "go to" people to get things done. People were tired. Morale was low. They had been in storm for a long time.

We worked with some of the teams and asked them to describe how they saw things, showing them the Tuckman model and asking them to locate their own team within it. This process was somehow therapeutic, with people realizing that actually there was a way out of the storming stage. It just needed some refreshed thinking on their part, and the application of some situational leadership.

The Situational Leadership model was put forward by Paul Hersey and Ken Blanchard in the 1960s and has become widely accepted in management science and forms a cornerstone of many leadership development programs. It proposes four leadership styles that we have summarized as "Tell," "Sell," "Participate," and "Delegate," with a theory that leaders should adopt the right style for their team, depending on the needs of their team. Hersey and Blanchard discuss the teams' needs in a slightly different way to the manner we have used in this text, but there is logic to that as will hopefully become clear. Their excellent model, in full, talks about the maturity level of the team and how this influences leadership behavior. In our practice we see that this approach fits neatly alongside the Form, Storm, Norm, Perform model of team development proposed by Bruce Tuckman with some very practical outcomes.

The four leadership styles of Telling, Selling, Participating, and Delegating necessitate different behaviors. Under the Telling approach, the leader acts to direct the group. In this he or she must be clear and unambiguous. In SPECTRUM terms a strong slug of red behavior is required. This telling stage is not very collaborative and there is little consultation. The leader states what s/he wants to happen, and the team does it.

Under the Selling style the team members are still directed by the leader and there is more engagement. It is also likely that the team will need to be convinced of the direction being proposed (and the leader's role may also be questioned). In this stage the leader must convince some of the team members of the course of action to follow and make the team understand the benefits of doing things in a specific way. This will require yellow and green behaviors to paint a view of the future and to encourage connection and collaboration to get there.

The Participating leader comes closer to the group and to build relationships while integrating becoming part of the team. In this stage the leader is less directive and more consulting. In SPECTRUM terms he or she will be using a much softer "green" style to encourage the group to step up and follow their own intuition and knowledge, so much so that the leader might not be the prime decision maker any more, as this is beginning to be transferred to the group.

This transference is completed in the fourth and final stage "Delegating" in which the leader passes on most of the responsibilities for decision making and task management of a given project or task to various members of the team, relying on their skill and experience to make the best decisions. This is a nirvana state for most leaders, whose role can then shift to looking at broader issues such as strategy and vision.

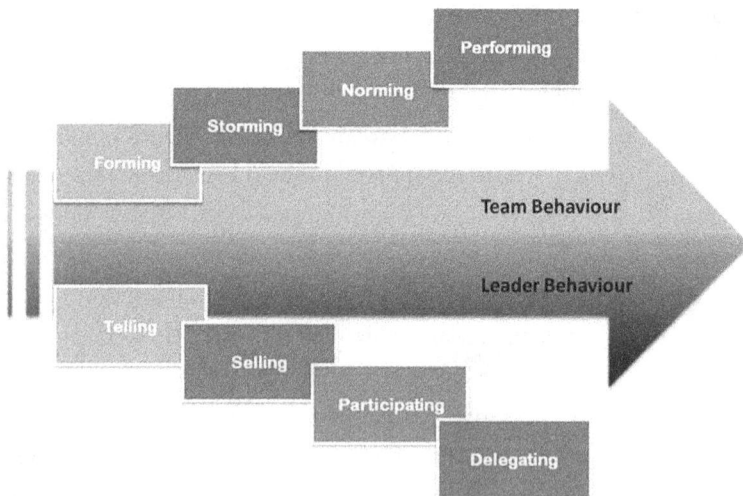

As a manager and leader you can run the Hersey and Blanchard model alongside the Tuckman model with good effect. When the team is "forming," the leader is best advised to give more direction and adopt a "telling" style. When a team first forms the roles and purpose of the team and the individuals in it can be unclear, and what is needed in this situation is for the leader to show a clear purpose and direction. The leader at this stage must tell the people what needs to be done. This is also important when launching any new initiative where the leader must be certain to paint a picture of the future and a detailed directive on how to get there.

Once the team is formed and has knowledge of their task then the leadership focus needs to shift. The team is now "storming," vying for position and trying to forge a direction with an emerging sense of identity. Storming is a stressful place to be. It is a state in which outcomes are uncertain and the internal focus can be overwhelming. Constant personnel changes are a common feature at this stage and the change in dynamic that each one of these changes brings with it ensures that the tensions in the group remain high.

So, the role of the leader at this stage is different. Here the leader creates a common vision to help move the team to the next phase but must recognize that this storming must be allowed to play out before the team can move to the next stage. His or her role is still very much to be out in front, and to provide a beacon from which others can take position.

Maintaining a directive style at this stage risks micromanaging the team and this will stifle creativity, decision making, and, ultimately, output and effort. Instead, the leader might adopt an approach where the benefits are underlined.

In the final stage the team is mature, and all members are able to work to a high standard and self-manage. At this stage the leader can allow the team to self-manage their issues, although he or she must be alert to issues raised and be able to act as champion for team members who need support. The chances are that by the time the team reaches this stage each person in it is highly competent and is most likely to be operating at one of the higher levels of Maslow's pyramid. The independence of the team allows the leader to focus much more on longer term strategy and direction.

Team leader should...*

Forming* - stage 1

High dependence on leader for guidance and direction. Little agreement on team aims other than received from leader. Individual roles and responsibilities are unclear. Leader must be prepared to answer lots of questions about the team's purpose, objectives and external relationships.

TELL

Team are unsure of what needs to happen. Leader uses a telling style to provide lots of structure and direction. Must show support to allow growth

Storming – stage 2

Decisions don't come easily within group. Team members vie for position as they attempt to establish themselves in relation to other team members and the leader. Clarity of purpose increases but plenty of uncertainties persist. Cliques and factions form and there may be power struggles.

SELL

Team is internally focussed. Leader builds confidence, praises and reinforces the ground rules. Encourages more autonomy. Hold boundaries.

Norming – stage 3

Agreement and consensus is largely formed among team. Roles and responsibilities are clear and accepted. Big decisions are made by group agreement. Smaller decisions may be delegated to individuals or small teams within group. Commitment and unity is strong.

PARTICIPATE

Team are used to the task and have established a working pattern. Leader involves team in decisions, welcomes ideas and creates independence within the team. Individuals develop.

Performing – stage 4

The team is more strategically aware; the team knows clearly why it is doing what it is doing. The team has a shared vision and is able to stand on its own feet with no interference or participation from the leader. There is a focus on over-achieving goals, and the team makes most of the decisions against criteria agreed with the leader. The team has a high degree of autonomy.

DELEGATE

Team are comfortable, want to share leadership and have the skills to do so. Leader gives new responsibilities and spends time co-ordinating.

*Team stages from Tuckman and leadership approaches From Hersey & Blanchard's Situational Leadership Model

At each level, the concept of personal leadership is crucial. Through your own skills, actions, and behaviors you will personally represent and demonstrate the things that are important. Your own actions will speak more loudly than your words. This is why leadership is so carefully linked to branding. As we saw with the example of Ted and Selima from the previous chapter it is not easy to provide leadership in an area that is not in line with your passion. In short, if you cannot speak passionately about the things that you feel are important then you cannot expect to demonstrate leadership in this area. We have come across this many times in business: The divisional boss who is feeling at personal odds to the strategic directions being given by the board will find it hard to lead his team through a change program. Instead of supporting the initiative with positive language he will, without really thinking about it, give off signs of dissonance and apathy. We can all spot these signs. You must be able to put yourself behind these changes 100 percent for your energy (positive and negative) will be highly contagious.

Use Listening Leader adapted from Work by Clementine and Emilio Galli Zugaro, Shane Safir and Michael Fullen

The Listening Leader

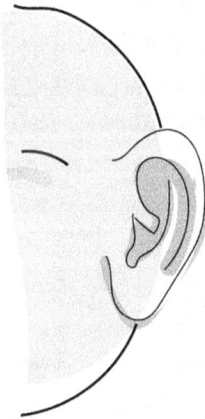

L **Look and Listen:**
Observe everything you can first hand. You have two ears, two eyes but only one mouth so uses them in that ration.

I **Involve to Others:**
Talk to others. Ask open questions of the lowest people not just your direct reports. Work with cross functional & diagonal slices of employees not just the senior teams

S **Share Ideas:**
Share Ideas with others and allow others to share their ideas with you. Give them feedback even if your answer is no & tell them why!

T **Time:**
Give others your time, make time for yourself to plan and think. Time is the only non-renewable resource, it ticks on a second at a time and can never be replaced once lost. Have a forward focus.

E **Empathy:**
Be in tune with how others feel and behave try to understand it from their perspective. Never jump to conclusions. Give credit.

N **Now and Next:**
Plan what is next? Where does the focus need to be now to get to the best future? Delegate it, empower others to solve it!

The LISTEN acronym provides a useful template of how to lead others.
Look and Listen: Observe everything you can first hand. Listen, you have two ears and two eyes but only one mouth, so use them in that split: twice as much looking and twice as much listening as talking.
Involve Others: Talk to others, ask open questions of the lowest people not just your direct reports. Work with cross-functional diagonal slices of employees, not just the senior teams.
Share Ideas: Work with others and allow others to share their ideas with you, give them feedback even if your answer is no! Tell them why!
Time: Give others your time, make time for yourself to plan and think. Time is the only nonrenewable resource, it ticks on a second at a time and can never be replaced once lost. Have a forward focus.

Empathy: Be in tune with how others feel and behave; try to understand it from their perspective. Never jump to conclusions. Give credit.

Now and Next: Plan what is next. Where does the focus need to be now to get to the best future? Delegate it, empower others to solve it!

Using the SPECTRUM Model to Understand

Your own style as a leader is based on your Spectrum Behavioral Profile. At various stages of team development, the leader of any team or business will be required to instill mission and purpose, drive action, make decisions, solve problems, delegate tasks, give feedback and disseminate information, and more besides. Each individual leader will have a way of doing this based on his or her behavioral profile. Those preferences are discussed in the illustration of leadership styles using the different behavior profiles.

Leadership functions	Leadership styles			
	Green	Red	Blue	Yellow
Instilling mission and purpose	Reminding everyone of shared values	Telling people what to achieve	Studying situation and explaining relevance of goals	Building consensus about what people want
Driving action	Inspiring people with a vision of possibilities	Expressing urgency and pressing for higher achievement	Providing a plan and monitoring compliance	Showing people how to get what they want
Making decisions	Collaborating with others or referring decisions upward	Swiftly choosing a clear course of action	Thoroughly reviewing what's involved and then deciding	Announcing but perhaps revising depending on reactions
Solving problems	Encouraging group participation	Acting independently or consulting with experts	Analyzing data, evaluating options, and proceeding step-by-step	Experimenting and exploring possibilities
Delegating tasks	Trusting subordinates, showing patience, and reviewing if needed	Assuming competence and providing minimal supervision	Giving detailed instructions and reviewing periodically	Inviting others to take on tasks and reviewing informally

Leadership functions	Leadership styles			
	Green	Red	Blue	Yellow
Giving feedback	Focusing on needs for improvement or failures to meet the highest standards	Rewarding successes and pointing out failures	Assessing performance objectively	Offering frequent positive remarks
Communicating information	Sharing and requesting information to keep in touch	Giving and asking only when needed	Providing and requiring a lot of regular documentation	Keeping in touch informally

Each behavioral preference will approach these tasks in a different way. The key takeaway is that great leaders have to show all four main colors and that all four can still be seen as inspirational—it isn't just one color that leads!

Let's look at the leadership styles of each color profile in a bit more detail.

The GREEN Leader

Goal: To earn the respect of others—they would like to be seen as living up to personal ideals.

Philosophy: If only they live according to the ethical rules and try hard, behave in a principled and ethical way, they will be rewarded. It is important for them to cooperate with those committed to significant goals of value—to live up to the standards of the group with whom they identify.

Leadership Attitudes and Behavior
- Looks at the long-range benefits of work projects
- Is serious in approach
- Tries best to adhere to organizational goals and values, to follow the expectations and directions of higher-level leaders
- Strives to be the very best leader possible
- Shows respect for higher-level leaders—expects them to model desired behavior
- Uses an idealistic and nonlinear thinking mode

- Believes leadership failures are one's own fault
- Values patience as a leader
- Wants higher-level leaders to take an interest in his/her development
- Desires coaching and guidance from higher-level leaders—provides the same for followers
- Wants followers to participate in problem-solving discussions
- Cooperates with other leaders and expects the same for his/her team
- Willing to delegate with trust and patience
- Behaving in an ethical way and insisting on that behavior from one's staff
- Have high expectations of performance for team but may not be explicit—feedback may emphasize critical reviews
- Wants to follow a higher-level leader who provides encouragement and support

The RED Leader

Goal: To be seen as competent and capable.
Philosophy: If you want to succeed, you have to help yourself. Take advantage of opportunities. Take risks for the sake of mastery. It's important for you to believe in yourself.

Leadership Attitudes and Behavior
- Needs to see the tangible payoffs from actions
- Wants freedom to do as they want to get desired results
- Uses crisp and terse directions—provides clear goals
- Is confident, and in command of the situation—desires working for those who exhibit the same characteristics
- Provides and wants immediate feedback
- Is explicit about what is wanted
- Demands and will accept only successful performance
- Delegates to those who are competent, requiring minimal supervision
- Expects prompt responsiveness
- Doesn't accept excuses readily
- Keeps decision-making in own hands, except in areas where he/she lacks expertise—then desires expert help

- Expects to be immediately apprised of problems, along with recommendations for solutions
- Provides and expects direct and open communications

The BLUE Leader

Goal: To be viewed as a solid thinker and performer—to be seen as cautious and responsible.

Philosophy: Think before you act. Consolidate what you know and avoid mistakes. "Be sure rather than be sorry."

Leadership Attitudes and Behavior

- Needs to see the overall framework
- Structure is important—prefers explicit directions, policies, and procedures
- Needs to know rationales for procedures
- Desires to see new leadership build on old knowledge
- Wants to know things in depth, willing to spend a lot of time to learn details before acting
- Likes higher-level leaders to be organized and knowledgeable
- Develops explicit progress yardsticks for assessment
- Provides objective criticism and desires the same
- Functions in a disciplined way
- Will desire to see justifications, specific examples, and data that support orders and recommendations
- Doesn't like to be rushed—desires time to do things right
- Asks questions about specific information

The YELLOW Leader

Goals: To be liked, to be an accepted member, to fit in, and to receive acknowledgment.

Philosophy: Adapt to new situations. Learn how to gain acceptance from others. Be alert and aware of new things, experimenting with them to keep ahead of others. Be sensitive to people and to organizational politics.

Leadership Attitudes and Behavior
- The working atmosphere and the personal relationship are important—likes to be friends with everyone
- Enjoys doing things with others
- Seeks opportunities to have a starring or prominent role
- Uses positive feedback and encouragement
- Likes to explore new possibilities
- Is flexible in ways of dealing with people
- Has a positive self-attitude
- Favors creative solutions
- Provides encouragement and acknowledgment
- Emphasizes group morale and identification
- Uses intuitive and nonlinear thinking processes
- Is empathetic and tactful when dealing with staff
- Is able to keep perspective when he/she has erred
- Uses persuasive selling to influence others to follow

When things are not going well the different style will again have preferences and strengths to bring to the table to handle different situations in different ways.

ADVERSE CONDITIONS When Things Are Not Going Well: GREEN Leaders

Stress
- Encourages suggestions from staff and others
- Provides information to everyone affected
- Reminds people of responsibility for resolving issues
- Emphasizes team cooperation
- Uses inspirational examples
- May become overdependent on advice from others
- May lose confidence in abilities
- May complain a lot and find fault

Conflict
- Listens attentively to others
- Tries to give others what they want

ADVERSE CONDITIONS When Things Are Not Going Well: RED Leaders

Stress

- Takes charge and provides direction
- Becomes actively involved in all areas
- Is demanding and insistent on immediate response
- Spot checks progress
- Disciplines for failure to show improvement
- Can change direction fast when solutions do not work
- Will not rest until source of stress is removed
- Tries to solve problems independently
- May become somewhat frantic in behavior
- May become irritable and angry
- Efforts may become diffused trying to do much personally

Conflict Style

- Argues confidently and strongly for his/her position
- Will not give up until gains what is wanted
- Presses opponent to justify arguments
- Wants swift resolution of differences
- Can express feelings as well as ideas
- Finds conflict stimulating
- Once issue is settled prefers to move on
- Encourages expression of differences but wants argument to cease once a decision has been made
- May become overly coercive
- May make situations overly combative—"win the battle" but lose the war

ADVERSE CONDITIONS When Things Are Not Going Well: BLUE Leaders

Stress

- Analyze sources of difficulty at great length
- Will be critical of loose structures or inadequate explanations or failure to pay attention to details

- Will slow decision-making until assured the right solution has been found
- Plan efforts in detailed fashion with roles and responsibilities clearly delineated
- Will use control systems, budgets, and schedules
- Will review progress periodically
- May fail to respond to emergency in time
- May not focus on broader issue—overly analyze
- May supervise so closely that resentment is created

Conflict Style
- Responds in a calm and deliberate fashion
- Gathers facts and provides logical and organized argument
- Will not give in unless presented with better facts and logic
- Reviews issues systematically
- Refuses to engage in emotional exchanges
- Prefers to wait until issues are fully understood before making a decision
- May get too involved in details and ignore broader issue
- May ignore emotional and feeling factors
- May seem overly resistant and stubborn

ADVERSE CONDITIONS When Things Are Not Going Well: YELLOW Leaders

Stress
- Will try to see the positive side of what is happening
- Will be encouraging and supportive of staff
- Emphasizes looking for innovative solutions
- Forecasts optimistic outcomes
- Keeps aware of organizational concerns
- Personally, visits people at work
- May diffuse focus by trying out too many solutions
- May create credibility problems if forecasts are not realized
- May not correct poor performance in time

Conflict Style
- Is friendly and tries to minimize differences
- Listens empathetically and shows understanding
- Seeks to find a mutually satisfactory resolution
- If faced with unpleasant consequence uses a positive appeal to gain what is desired
- Doesn't use demeaning or critical comments
- May lose out because of unwillingness to confront
- May seem to lack principle—or confuse others concerning real position
- May fail to deal with emotional issues

Often a leader's style is revealed in the way that they speak. For instance:

Green leaders might say
"I believe that one leads best if one can develop a meaningful vision of our work and its value."

"I strive to create an atmosphere where everyone on the team feels his/her contribution is desired and valued."

"I feel that if we share in the decision-making process there will be greater commitment to achieving our objectives."

"I believe in delegating as much responsibility as possible and trust the integrity and dedication of my employees to handle things effectively."

"I believe in living up to the same standards I hold for others."

"I make myself available to provide help and assistance, to provide developmentally significant experiences to help their professional growth."

"I hold frequent meetings for sharing information and expect subordinates to keep me informed as much as possible. In turn, I try to keep my bosses aware of what is happening...."

"When people propose new ideas to me, I usually ask: Whom will it benefit? Does it fit our goals and values? Is it something of value for the long term? Are our ideas of interest to you? Will it represent our very best?"

Red leaders might say

"It is up to me to state what our objectives are and assign tasks accordingly to achieve them."

"I expect competence and responsiveness to issues. I will only interfere if the job is not being executed competently."

"I want people to act independently unless they are encountering difficulty and I expect them to report those difficulties immediately, along with recommendations for dealing with them."

"I am forthright and direct in my comments. I expect the same from my staff. I want them to argue for what they believe, but to stop that once I have made a decision."

"I want our organization to be able to take advantage of opportunities as they occur."

"What counts for me is getting things done."

"I don't like spending time on idle chit chat."

"I expect people to be direct, brief, and to the point."

"Most of the time I expect people to be able to solve their own problems."

"I stand behind my people and fight for them."

"When I ask questions, I want to know: What will be the bottom-line payoff? Is it something we can readily implement? Who needs to do what and when? What opportunity does it represent?"

Blue leaders might say

"I believe the best way to lead is to have a clear idea of what is expected and wanted and to be able to communicate that to your staff."

"I spend time and energy to work in a planned and organized way and I expect the same of those who work for me."

"I want to minimize risk and loss and expect people to weigh risks and benefits, keep track of expenses, and report accurately on events."

"I do not want any surprises; therefore, I expect complete information at regularly scheduled intervals. Reports have to be timely and accurate."

"Proposals must be well documented, supported by facts and figures, and be organized in a systematic way."

"I believe in keeping track of what is happening and schedule reviews to make sure everything is progressing satisfactorily."

"I believe in treating people fairly and objectively. I provide them with clear policies and procedures to avoid misunderstanding."

"The quality of thinking is very important to me. I don't expect people to do something without justification."

"I use meetings to inform and be informed. They are conducted in an orderly fashion, notes are taken and distributed to everyone, action plans are documented with starting time, reporting times, and estimated time of completion."

"The questions that are on my mind are: What's the rationale for doing this? What are the facts and details? Exactly how are we going to get this done? Is this consistent with our policies and procedures?"

Yellow leaders might say

"I believe in maintaining high morale among the people who work with me. I strive to get to know each of them personally, provide acknowledgment for their contributions and to communicate positively about our goals, prospects, and achievements."

"When people come to me I listen and respond empathetically, encouraging them to be open to alternatives."

"I try to be open myself to new ideas, give them a fair hearing, and explore possibilities. I encourage others to do the same, believe in using techniques like brainstorming to find creative approaches."

"I see myself as a moderator during conflicts, striving to build a climate where we can view differences as an opportunity to explore differences and to solve them in win–win ways."

"I value people who can get along well with others, who keep relationships smooth and can impress outsiders with their manner and performance."

"I devote time to understanding key people in the organization, building good relationships and being aware of special sensitivities. I keep in touch with those people, remember things about them, and always make sure to treat them well."

Remember These Golden Rules of Leadership

If you are the leader, EVERYTHING you say and everything you do matters.

Understand the NEEDS of others and understand that you will need to adopt a different style with each one.

Teams go through stages of development. Your role as leader will change as the needs of the team change.

USE the colors to help you apply the best leadership skills. Use RED to drive and make decisions, use BLUE to set processes and methodology. Use GREEN to feedback and coach. Use YELLOW to inspire, show positivity embrace change, build networks and energize people around you.

CHAPTER 4

O Is for Opportunities

Can You Take Advantage of the Opportunities That Will Grow Your Business?

"Opportunities like islands don't come to you, you must swim out to them!"

—Anon

An opportunity is a time or set of circumstances that make it possible to do something.

This chapter looks at networking and touches on marketing and sales. We find that many clients struggle to make initial contacts to get the opportunity to grow their network and sell their products. Many of us are poor at managing the sales and marketing pipeline. This chapter will give a few pointers for tools, tips, techniques, and models that can help improve your success at following up on the opportunities you have to sell and get your name out there.

Networking is regarded by many as a dirty word. It is rare to come across people who actually enjoy networking. For most of us it is a necessary evil that we go through to grow ourselves professionally and to secure business. Our reluctance to do it (in the UK at least) seems to stem from a feeling of falseness that is associated with it. This is because for some reason people think that they have to behave differently to have a great networking experience. This may or may not be true.

Why Would You Notice Me?

Part of the problem with networking goes back to our primeval history. There is a wonderful TED talk by Dr. Mark Bowden that was delivered at the TEDX event in Toronto in 2013. In a wonderfully engaging presentation (well, what else would you expect from an expert in body language!), Bowden set down some of the key principles about behavior and body language that are particularly relevant when it comes to networking. The impact that the speech had on me was to make me realize the importance of the messages that we "flash" across the room at each other. At the risk of dreadfully dumbing down Bowden's speech (which is available on YouTube by the way) I will summarize these for you now.

In short, when we first set eyes on another person our primeval brain kicks in and runs through a simple process. This process goes broadly as follows:

1. Is this person a potential predator (i.e., a threat to me)?
2. Is this person a potential sexual partner (i.e., a mate for me)?
3. Is this person a potential ally or friend (i.e., someone I want in my group)?

The brain runs through this sequence faster at lightning speed and before we've even realized we've done it. At each stage it processes information received and if it runs through the process without getting to "yes" then it comes to a simple conclusion. If the other person is not a predator, not a sexual partner, and not a friend, then we regard them with *indifference*. When you think about it, that's quite an insulting term. If you are indifferent to me then presumably you don't really care if I am there or not. You probably don't really notice me, and you certainly aren't going to be excited to engage with me at networking events.

If Bowden is right then this can explain why so many of us hate networking. For many introverts in particular those moments spent in the coffee area of exhibitions and conferences are painfully uncomfortable. In these situations our body language becomes closed, nervous, and insecure and we probably give off messages that read "I don't want to be here." In Bowden's view, we aren't giving off any signals that present us as a predator, partner, or friend.

Predator messages are easy to spot. Just imagine a velociraptor has walked into the room. Stern face, closed eyebrows, bared teeth, aggressive movements all contrive to make other people disengage. Nobody wants to talk to a crazed carnivore. Potential sexual partner postures are perhaps more fun to imagine, but again they are not really the sort of body language you want to be giving off at networking soirees, although we can probably all think of people who do. Outward signs of sexual availability certainly make people memorable, but it's not professional and might even be immoral. What you need to be giving off, Bowden argues, are "friend" messages, because then others will want to engage with you and can be focused on whatever discussion we have to share.

What do we mean by "friend" messages? The most obvious example of this is the eyebrow flash. Imagine you're on a crowded commuter train and you see a friend get on. He is further down the carriage from you and too far away to speak. What do you do? You raise your eyebrows in a flash of recognition. This is the universal sign for friend. Combine it with a smile, a genuine one that includes your eyes and not one that is solely signaled with the mouth and you are sending friend messages. Bowden argues we should be sending more friend messages. So perhaps what we need is to accept that a little change in behavior can have big changes in our experiences. By flashing subtle friend messages with our eyebrows, we might expect to engage in more profitable conversations. This flash also necessitates looking up and at people by the way, both of which are signs of confidence and are, in themselves, also more likely to encourage people to engage.

Networking with EDGE

But what about when the conversation starts—how do you network effectively? We coach people in the use of what we call the EDGE method of networking. This stands for ENGAGE, DEVELOP, GO FOR IT, EXIT.

This approach starts with the ENGAGE phase. This is where you flash the friend messages and make those first introductions. Our advice here

NETWORKING
WITH

ENGAGE   DEVELOP   GO FOR IT!   EXIT

is to be approachable; look up, look happy, and use open body language. Look interested and respond to questions that others ask you. There is a saying that to be interesting you have to be interested. This makes sense and certainly seems to work. Ask lots of questions to get to break the ice. Give the other person something to respond to. Use simple introductory question such as, "Have you come far?" "What brings you here?" Maybe you can spot a "Haven't we met before at. . .?" Or "What a splendid umbrella, where did you get it?"

Another approach might be to develop a reason from the environment you're in—"It's always crowded here isn't it? I hope the coffee's worth the wait."

While all this is going on stay positive, build rapport, and smile. Hold eye contact at a comfortable level (don't stare them out).

You can now build the conversation and move into the DEVELOP stage of the conversation. One REALLY good exercise to develop your networking and conversational skills is to use a three- or five-questions technique. Asking somebody five open[1] questions in a row will allow you to really get to the nub of an issue. Try it. Find a friend and ask them an open question. Then, while they are talking, make sure that the next thing that comes out of your mouth is another open question that builds upon what they just said to you. It's a powerful approach that can be used in coaching. In networking we'd suggest cutting it down to just three

---

[1]Open questions are questions that cannot be answered with a single word but that require a longer sentence. Good examples of open questions include "What," "How," and "Why" (although be careful with why as it can also be accusatory).

questions at the maximum; you don't want it to become an interrogation. It's a really useful method to help you to find common ground.

With the conversation now well underway you can enter the GO FOR IT! stage. This is why you are here after all, so just go for it. It is your chance to get what you want from the conversation. Sometimes you have to be bold enough to just ask straight out what you want. For example, if you want to arrange a follow-up meeting to talk to them about working together in the future you might say, "That's really interesting, we have lots of common ground and it's an area we have real expertise in. Perhaps I could come and see you next week?" If you've done the first two stages well the answer should be favorable.

With the appointment or follow-up secured the next thing is to get out. You've got what you came for so get out now before they change their mind! This is the EXIT phase.

Exchange business cards and contact details, offer to connect up on social media (even if they said no to you before this will give you another route in for a second try). Then, make your excuses and leave. A nice way to do this is to ask them who else they would like to speak to while in the session and maybe help them with a few introductions. Doing that will definitely reinforce the "friend" message.

As you grow your network and build your presence you are going to need a simple tool to help you manage your growing customer database.

Introducing the Cooker

The Cooker: A way to think about handling clients, leads and opportunities

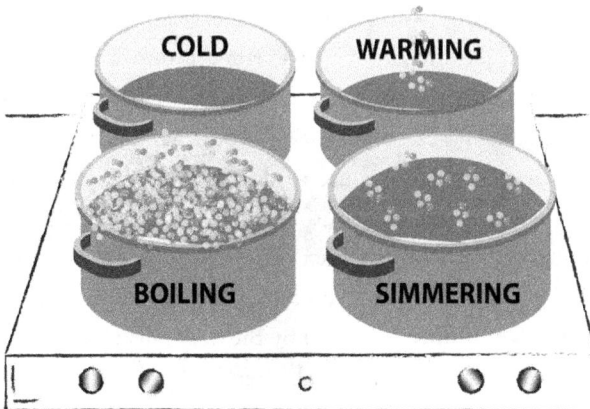

We use the cooker model as a way to manage leads, clients, and opportunities. It is not a very complicated model; in fact it is possibly the simplest model of relationship management that you will ever see. In this model, if possible we split our leads and clients into four separate categories, managing each category in a different way.

The model works like this. Imagine a typical kitchen stove, hob, or cooker that has four rings on which pots and pans may be placed. Imagine that on each of these four positions sits a pan. The first pan, situated at the back left of the hob, is cold. It has no heat under it. Next to that stands another one, on a low heat, just warming nicely. The third pot, at the front right, is simmering nicely, but is not at the boil. The final pot, situated at front left, is boiling. Each of these pots represents a group of your clients, leads, opportunities, and projects. Some will be stone cold, not even knowing of your existence, some will be aware of you and just starting to engage with you about what you might do or how your product might help them. Another group will be more engaged, and while they have not taken the plunge, they are very close to working with you and on the verge of buying. The final group will be people and projects you are working on today, your current clients and customers. The analogy with the model is very straightforward.

The Cold Pot

The cold pot represents the wider marketplace. It is all the potential people that could be interested in your product. If you want to talk the language of business plans then this is your market size, the population of people ready to engage with products and services of the type you have to offer. What you have to do of course is reach out to them. Think of your business. Who is in your cold pot? Who or what are the people that you need to be reaching out to? How will you reach out to them? What methods and channels will you use to do that? How can you network with them? Where do they "hang out" so that you can mix with them and expose them to you and your product or service? What are they seeking? What problems do they have that you can solve? Your ability to reach into this pot will be significantly impacted by the decisions you make around branding that we saw in the earlier chapter. If they see some benefit in working with you or buying your product then you can move them from the cold pot to the warm pot.

How do you gain attention? Well, this question is the focus of your Marketing Plan (if you didn't know you had one then read on and you soon will). What you do here dovetails with the work you have already put in under branding. These days clients are reached in many ways, the most ubiquitous and (arguably) easiest is online. Your brand thinking needs to be supported by some targeted marketing designed to appeal to the people in your cold pot. The more you know about your cold pot the easier this will be. Successful approaches will paint a picture of an experience or show how your business can solve a problem that the target audience has. Chances are this will involve clever use of images (first) and words (secondary) to generate interest. Whatever your product or service it will likely be something that helps the consumer in some way. Perhaps by saving time, money, or effort, which allows them to bypass a block or helps them to overcome menial, repetitive tasks. Whatever the benefit is, it needs to be communicated to the customer, so they can see exactly how it will help them. If you are completely stuck for this, we would suggest using Features Advantages and Benefits. This involves setting out in a simple way what the features of your offering are (you can pick this from the work you've done on branding in an earlier chapter). Next, describe the advantages of using your product or service. And finally outline the benefits of using your product or service. If you know your product and your market well, then this should be a straightforward task. If you do not know the product or market well, then that might explain any troubles that you are having moving your potential clients into the warm pot.

The Warm Pot

These represent the businesses or buyers that have already noticed you. This might mean a number of things, from clicking a "like" on social media to downloading a file or maybe even just having worked with you before. All your personal contacts, LinkedIn connections, Facebook friends, etc., are in this pot at least. And from here they should only go in one direction. How can you do that? This is where effective sales prospecting and customer relationship systems can come into play. How will we gain their interest? What is our content strategy? Social proof available to back up our reputation? How do we make this information available and where? Is it on a website, via videos, or customer ratings? It is a cardinal sin in business to allow any lead to fall from warm to cold. Think for a minute what that means when that happens. When a lead goes from warm to cold they are no longer aware of you, no longer receiving your marketing updates. They are closed to you and you're going to have to work hard (maybe doubly hard) to win them back. But does this happen? Yes, it can do, and it can do a lot. How this happens is simple. You have a contact working at Company A. Let's call her Kelly. Now, Company A has always bought the odd thing from you, and Kelly is firmly in your warm pot. You know that she is there, working away at her job, and you know that in a year or so she'll be back to buy from you again, moving quickly through the simmering pot and into the boiling pot. But let's suppose that that time comes and goes with no purchase. When you realize this, you e-mail Kelly. Then, when she doesn't reply to your e-mail you tentatively phone her up, slightly nervous now about why she hasn't done any business with you or responded to your approaches. You call is answered by a fellow introducing himself as Rex, who tells you that Kelly left 6 months ago to go to Company B. Rex is delighted to speak with you, but he's already in a deal with an old contact to get what Company A needs from them. You ask if anyone has Kelly's contact details. Sadly, nobody has.

It's a common story and one that can be prevented with good stakeholder management and a firm control over the cooker. You need to be staying close to Kelly not just taking it for granted that she will be back. By staying in regular touch and fostering a close relationship with Kelly you could actually have come out of that scenario with completely the opposite outcome. How? Well, by keeping close to Kelly you'd get early news that she was leaving. This would enable you to engage with her about where she was going next, and whether or not there would be any way that you could support her in her new role. You might need to offer a sweetener here, but most people are keen to keep the same contacts because it shows their new employer that they have an effective and established network. Then, given the knowledge that Kelly was due to leave you might have enticed her to do business with you via Company A before she went to Company B. Alternatively you could work with her to get an early introduction to Rex to ensure that you maintained the business with Company A and built a relationship with him early, before he decided to use another supplier. With the sale to Company A in the bag, and a strong connection on Company B now in hand (because you've been close to Kelly), it's quite likely that you can generate two sales whereas in the initial example you sold a grand total of nothing.

This classic example demonstrates the huge investment of personal time and energy that goes on with the cooker. Maintaining many relationships is hard, and harder for some behavior profiles than others.

The Simmering Pot

The simmering pot contains all the businesses or clients who are actively engaging with you and who are on the verge of a sale. You need to treat this group very carefully and very personally. A prime skill that you will need to manage all four hobs of the cooker is listening, and this is especially true for the leads and connections that are in the simmering pot. Treat them wrong, and they can go cold very quickly, but treat them right, and give them the right messages and, even more crucially, the right experience and you can take the limit off what they might then spend.

The Boiling Pot

The boiling pot contains the businesses and individual customers that you are dealing with today. They are the clients with whom you have a confirmed engagement and from whom you will receive payment. It goes without saying that this group needs particular care, you want them to have an "on brand" experience that keeps them coming back for more. You need to think what you can do to go the extra mile. What can you do above and beyond their expectations and give them the "WOW!" factor? An important part of the boiling pot is the opportunity for "upsell," taking an opportunity to enhance, upgrade an item being received, or selling an additional item or service that complements the first. Sales people love an upsell, from "supersize" meals at McDonalds to super wide wheel trims on your Aston Martin. If you are in the business of selling, you need to know what your upsell opportunities are and have them ready to be deployed when you see the signs that a customer will be receptive. Every business has a chance for an upsell. What's yours?

If you're involved in sales or marketing your job is simple: To move your clients through the pots from Cold to Boiling. There are plenty of decisions to be made along the way, not least of which is how many clients or customers can you keep in the boiling pot? In other words, how many projects, clients, or customers can you be satisfying at any one time.

If you sense a block in your system, then you need to investigate ways you can remove the block as soon as possible. For instance, if no businesses are moving through your cold pot and into your warming pot, why is that? What you are seeing in this example is that clients are not being made aware of you, or if they are, then they are showing no evidence of that. At first sight this would appear to be a marketing block. Are you reaching out to these potential customers? If so, how? And what is it about that line of approach that isn't working? Are you targeting the wrong people, using the wrong methods, overly relying on one method, etc., etc., etc. Then, if leads are not moving from warm to simmering, it may be the sales process that is at fault. What you are seeing here is that potential customers are seeing your business as an option but are not moving forward in their desire to work with you. Why is that? Is that down to sales technique, marketing messages that don't quite fit the brand (do the brand and the behaviors fit?)? And if you are able to get customers into the simmering pot but are not able to entice them into the boiling pot what does that tell you about your ability to close sales? And what about the clients that are in the boiling pot, the ones that are actually generating today's pay check? What's going on there? Is there a large element of repeat business, whereby clients move in and out of the hot and simmering pot, or do they jump back into warm, or even cold when the job is done? If you are doing a good job and if you have the resources to handle it then keeping them in the boiling pot would be your ultimate goal. Some of this of course depends on your product or service, but most businesses would want to keep potential clients in boiling or, at worst, in simmering where they can quickly be brought to the boil.

The cooker model is a variant of the established AIDA model. The acronym stands for Attention, Interest, Desire (or decision), and Action and is attributed to advertising and sales pioneer Elias St. Elmo Lewis. It goes as far back as 1899, when Lewis talked about "catching the eye of the reader, to inform him, to make a customer of him." Within 10 years that had developed into "attract attention, awaken the interest, persuade and convince." These days there are many variants and derivatives of it, including the one that we have described here.

Marketing, Networking, and SPECTRUM

Our experience is that people with a high yellow content to their SPECTRUM profile make great networkers. These people are open communicators who are extroverted in nature and happy to reach out to others. Generally, the weakest performers in this area tend to have a higher blue element to their profile, preferring to communicate infrequently and in a way that isn't personal (i.e., e-mail). Blues it seems would much rather send an e-mail than use the phone. And it's a growing phenomenon.

When engaging with people face to face at networking events you will need to try to show more yellow behavior. Smiling, eye contact, asking questions, and being positive are all yellow. If you have lots of yellow in your profile then good for you, you won't find this hard but if you are low in yellow then you will find this challenging, draining, and stressful. The words I want to add on the end of that sentence are "at first." When you first try it this will feel unnatural, but this is where you must persevere. Behavior change is possible and it often looks less uncomfortable from the outside than it feels on the inside. And changing your behavior does not change your personality (well, not in the short term at least), but it can radically affect the way that other people experience being in your company. And small behavior changes are possible without selling out on who you are. How do I know this? Easy. Just give a little smile, right now. Go on, do it.

There. You did it. You just changed your behavior. And without betraying your inner self.

Remember These Golden Rules for Managing Opportunities

Networking is your friend. There are ways that you can get VALUE from these sessions.

Remember to flash FRIEND messages. Use open, friendly, and positive body language.

Network with EDGE to get the conversations that you want with the outcomes that you need: Engage, Develop, Go for it, and Exit.

Use your knowledge of SPECTRUM to mirror behaviors and build rapport.

Use the COOKER to grow and manage your customer base and combine it with your BRAND strategy to help keep your sales leads and clients engaged at all times.

CHAPTER 5

O Is for Outcomes

Are You Focused on the Right Outcomes to Hit Your Goals?

"To conquer frustration, one must remain intensely focused on the outcomes, not the obstacles."

—T.F. Hodge from "Within I Rise"

The outcome of an activity is the way that a thing turns out or the consequences of an action.

Our main focus in this chapter is on achieving the right outcomes in your job, and looking at ways of managing the performance of others to ensure the best outcomes. Ultimately, most jobs are assessed on their outcomes and outputs. That is, to what extent does the job holder deliver the key thing that is expected of the role? The output is the reason the job exists. As an individual in a role you should be able to state your key purpose. Why does your job exist? For a brain surgeon it may be to save lives, for a meter reader it may be to ensure accurate readings for billing, for a sales person it may be simply to earn revenue for the business. A key purpose or output should not be hard to define.

KEY OUTPUTS—Why Do We Do the Job?

We (you) are employed to deliver or produce ... (what) ... ?
As a job holder we are generally involved in a wide range of difficult and time-consuming activities and tasks which make up our day-to-day work. During periods of change and when resources are under pressure

it is more important than ever to think of our jobs in terms of results or "OUTPUTS." After all our success is not measured by how busy we are, but by our results! If you were paying all your staff out of your own pocket would you be happy to pay all of them for their current performance? Hopefully you would answer yes to most of your staff, but I am sure there would be one or two members of the team with a few question marks.

These outputs are known by many names, but we use the term Outputs. By defining our jobs in this way, we move from the list of activities that are normally included in our job descriptions toward a more results-oriented view of performance.

Once we know what we are trying to achieve in our jobs, then we can start to measure our success and decide how we should be spending our time to best effect.

So, for example, the management activity of "training" would become the output "more competent staff," or the activity "teambuilding" would be expressed in output terms as "High staff morale in the department." Outputs are linked to the job itself not the individual, so all chefs would have the outputs, but could have different terms, conditions, job descriptions, salaries, and goals.

Job Maps

To help us understand this a bit more we can use job maps. A job map is a diagram, created by you, that shows the interconnections between your job and the people who have an expectation of you in your job. It can be a very helpful tool for understanding and clarifying your role and priorities at work and as a tool for problem solving.[1] It is especially helpful when used as a tool to aid recruitment or to assist someone starting a new job.

A good job map can be used to:
- Give a clear indication of key responsibilities
- Make it clear to others exactly what it is that you do
- Identify and tackle problem areas
- Help produce a job description and be useful when setting objectives

---

[1]Job maps are also superb when used to create the job description and key outputs for a new role, allowing competencies and expectations to be quickly realized and easily shared.

When you combine your own map with the job maps of other people in your teams you may also be able to:

- Identify common problems
- Highlight areas where efforts are duplicated or confused
- Spot important new areas of work or gaps in existing responsibilities

How to Create Your Own Job Map

A job map is a simple diagram that looks a bit like a mind map. Take a large sheet of paper. In the middle of the page write your name and title. Then, dotted around the outside area of the page write the names or job titles of people or groups who have an expectation of you in your job.

When we explain this to groups we normally take the example of a nurse. In the center of the page we write nurse. Then, around the outside we write all the people that have an expectation of the nurse. Typically, these will be the patient, the patient's family, the ward sister, doctors, other nurses, porters, auxiliaries, the Royal College of Nursing, the hospital managers, and so on. You can go as deep as you want with this, but normally find that the top 8 to 10 stakeholders (because that's what these people or groups are) are enough to cover the key expectations. If you wish to explore the issues around your job more deeply then we'd also suggest placing more personal links on the page such as the nurse's own family and friends.

An example Job Map for a nurse

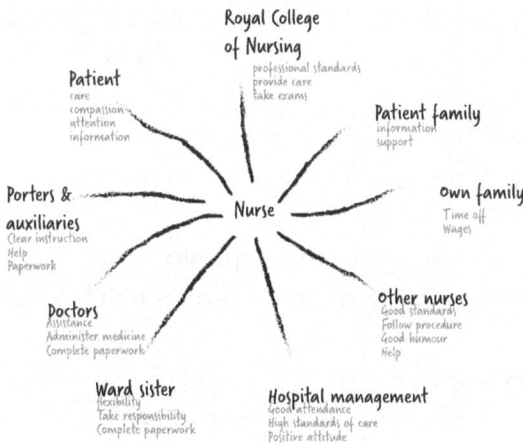

Royal College of Nursing
professional standards
provide care
take exams

Patient
care
compassion
attention
information

Patient family
information
support

Porters & auxiliaries
Clear instruction
Help
Paperwork

Nurse

own family
Time off
Wages

Doctors
Assistance
Administer medicine
Complete paperwork

other nurses
Good standards
Follow procedure
Good humour
Help

Ward sister
Flexibility
Take responsibility
Complete paperwork

Hospital management
Good attendance
High standards of care
Positive attitude

With that part completed, take a different colored pen and, under the names of the other parties, write what it is that they expect from the job holder. In the case of the nurse example, the patient might expect care, compassion, attention, and information. The patient's family might expect information and support, the doctor might expect professional standards, complete records, give medication as prescribed, etc. As you go around the paper you are building the key expectations for that role, and you are drawing up a charter of what "good" performance might look like. In the example of the nurse, "good" performance means giving all the stakeholders what they expect. What you will find by doing this is that there are lots more expectations placed upon us than we realize, and this might appear overwhelming. Not to deliver against the expectations of a third party is disappointing, but of course in the real world we must prioritize. Nevertheless, think of all the best nurses that you have known, and they somehow manage to deliver against all expectations. And so can you.

Sharing Your Job Map

Sharing the information in your job map is an important step in improving the understanding of how the various members in your team all rely on each other. Sharing your job map with your line manager and with other members of your team allows both of you to focus on your world and is a great way to help analyze where problems occur and where challenges can arise. Which of the various groups do you find the most difficult to deal with? What is the problem? What could be changed to make it better? If you can start to answer these questions, then you can really start to make progress toward improving performance.

When other people share their job map with you, think about what their job must be like. How can you help them to resolve their issues and challenges? How can they help you with yours? Can you develop a plan together?

Job maps are also great for solving problems with other groups. One really powerful approach is to arrange to meet with someone from your problem group and talk through your job map with them. Try to talk about the area where the problems arise and try to see the problem from their side. Focus on the issue and not personalities. Working with them in a collaborative way may help you both to get to the crux of the issue and lead to the best solution.

Using Job Maps to Understand Others

If it is not possible to talk the situation through with the problem group, then all is not lost. Take a few moments to draw a job map for your problem group. Which are the groups that they have to deal with? Where might their problems be? Could it be that the problem you experience is actually created by something that someone else expects of them? Looking at the problem from this perspective may enable you to see the other side of the problem. This can be a good place to look for solutions.

Combining Job Maps

If all members of a team can share their job maps, then you can get a very clear view of the full scope of responsibilities across the team. Spotlighting the problem areas will also give team leaders a really good view of where their staff face their major challenges. If we can look at this data from a higher level, then gaps or duplications of effort can also be spotted and common problem areas can be reviewed and targeted from a strategic perspective.

Using Your Job Map to Define Your Job Description

A job map can be a great skeleton for a job description. By working through a completed job map and placing an allocation of time against each expectation, you can begin to draw up a job description that can be helpful as part of both the recruitment and appraisal processes.

Defining Outputs and Outcomes with a Job Map

Looking at your job map for clues, try now to list what you consider to be the Key Outputs of your job. You can use your existing KRAs to help you, but they should be described here as single words, or short statements. In an ideal world, we would suggest that Pinpoint boards are used, a group of people with the same job are present, and at least one boss, other job map representatives and internal or external clients too.

Normally every job can be described by no more than five outputs. For example, a boss would have an output for Profit/Budget, Client Satisfaction, Team Management, Information and Client Retention, and possibly Growth.

A meter reader for the Southern Electricity Board could have just three outputs as follows—you will notice at this stage we are not qualifying the output by using how well, how much, or words like accurate, good, or high quality:

1. Meters Read
2. Provide Information
3. Portray a Company Image

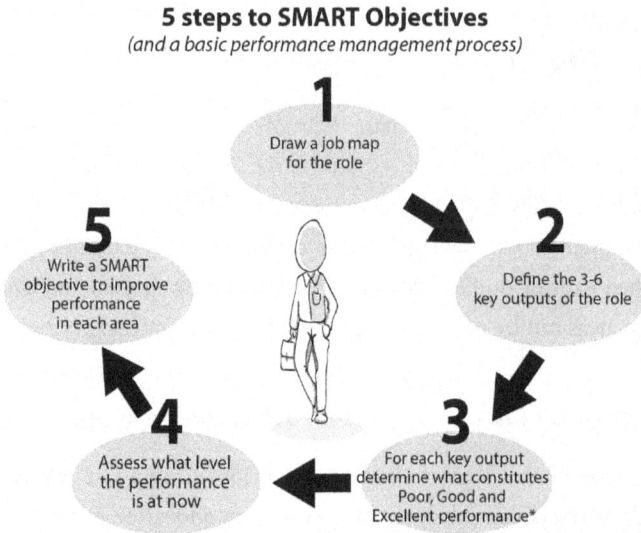

5 steps to SMART Objectives
(and a basic performance management process)

1
Draw a job map
for the role

2
Define the 3-6
key outputs of the role

3
For each key output
determine what constitutes
Poor, Good and
Excellent performance*

4
Assess what level
the performance
is at now

5
Write a SMART
objective to improve
performance
in each area

*You can also use Poor, Requires Improvement, Average,
Above Average, Good and Exceptional*

Setting Goals and Objectives

Great goals are SMART Goals

The idea of SMART goals was released into the world by George Doran, Arthur Miller, and James Cunningham in 1981. Since then, SMART goals have grown to be an essential tool in managing performance. The chances are that if you have ever been on any management or leadership training course then you will have heard something about setting SMART goals.

Setting SMART goals will enable you to clarify your ideas, focus your efforts, use your time and resources productively, and increase your chances of achieving what you want in life. SMART goals are:

Specific—Your goal should be clear and specific, so you know exactly what you're trying to achieve; otherwise, you won't be able to focus your efforts or feel truly motivated to achieve it. When drafting your goal, try to answer the five "W" questions:

- What do I want to accomplish?
- Why is this goal important?
- Who is involved?
- Where is it located?
- Which resources or limits are involved?

Measurable: It's important to have measurable goals, so that you can track your progress and stay motivated. Assessing progress helps you to stay focused, meet your deadlines, and feel the excitement of getting closer to achieving your goal.

Achievable: Your goal also needs to be realistic and attainable to be successful. In other words, it should stretch your abilities but still remain possible. When you set an achievable goal, you may be able to identify previously overlooked opportunities or resources that can bring you closer to it.

Realistic (or relevant): This step is about ensuring that your goal matters to you, and that it also aligns with other relevant goals. We all need support and assistance in achieving our goals, but it's important to retain control over them. So, make sure that your plans drive everyone forward, but that you're still responsible for achieving your own goal.

Time-Bound: Prioritize your goals to prevent everyday tasks from taking priority over your longer-term goals.

Setting Great Goals

Great goals are:

- Outcome focused: Once you understand your WHY (and it's an enthusiastic WHY) you're 90 percent there!

- In line with your values: The more a goal aligns with your inner or core values the EASIER it will be to achieve and the more energy you will feel when pursuing it. NOTE: We can achieve goals that don't align with our values but it's harder to do and less satisfying.
- Stated in the positive: That is, "I want healthy fingernails" rather than "I want to stop biting my nails."

It's really important when you are setting goals and objectives to keep an outcome focus.

The deeper you can dig into your thinking the more likely you are to set yourself a meaningful goal. Ask yourself:

- What is it that you really, REALLY want?
- What will it enable you to achieve? What is the SPECIFIC outcome you're looking for?
- What is your PAIN of NOT achieving your goal?

Keeping your goals aligned with your values will keep you authentic to your own wider ambitions and desires. Ask yourself:

- Is this goal in line with your life vision/overall life plan? (If you don't know, what does your gut tell you?)
- What's REALLY important to you in life? Will this goal help you achieve more of that?
- Are the goals something YOU truly want, or are they something you think you SHOULD have or SHOULD be doing? (Tip: If it is a SHOULD, it may be someone else's dream. . .)
- When you think about your goal does it give you a sense of deep contentment or "rightness," happiness and/or excitement? (If so, these are good signs that it's a healthy goal.)
- If you could have the goal RIGHT NOW would you take it? (If not, why not? What issues are there?)

Identifying Obstacles

If achieving your goal was simple, then you would have done it already. You need to know how you will identify and overcome the obstacles that stand between your goal.

O IS FOR OUTCOMES   73

Ask yourself:

- Who has control over this goal? Can YOU start and maintain this goal/outcome?
- Who else are you relying on?
- How will making this change affect other aspects of your life? (i.e., What else might you need to deal with?)
- What's good about your CURRENT SITUATION? (i.e., What's the benefit of staying right where you are?) Then ask, how can I keep those good aspects while STILL making this change?
- What might you have to give up/stop doing to achieve this goal?
- If there was something important around achieving this goal (to help you succeed, or that could get in the way) that you haven't mentioned yet, what would it be?
- WHO will you have to BE to achieve this goal?

Goal Size

Eating an elephant in one mouthful is not going to be easy. Ask yourself:

- Is your goal the right size to be working on?
- If it's too big, how can you break it down into smaller goals?
- If it's too small, how can you fit it into a larger goal?
- What would be the MINIMUM/Super-Easy level of goal to achieve?
- What would be your TARGET level of goal to achieve?
- What would be your EXTRAORDINARY level of goal to achieve?

Resources—Get Moving

You are going to need resources to get underway and achieve your goals. Ask yourself:

- What RESOURCES do you already have to help you achieve your goal? Make a list! (e.g., things, support from people, contacts, personal qualities, knowledge, skills, money, time, etc.).
- What RESOURCES do you NEED to help you achieve your goal? Make a list!

Ideas on managing people toward their goals.

Performance management is a book in itself. The reality is of course that many managers spend their time managing performance. In other words, they manage their team to ensure the people that work for them deliver their key outputs. If you are lucky you will have a team full of stars who excel at their roles (and if you follow the strategies laid out in this book we hope that's true!) but we also know that every now and then you will come across people who don't perform.

Attempts to tackle underperformance tend to have one of three possible outcomes:

Success: Concerted corrective action by managers and the employee combine to raise the standard of performance.

Failure (with grudging acceptance of the underperformance)

This all too frequent outcome occurs when management and the individual stop believing change is possible and the poor performance is tolerated as "just the way it is," leaving the person adrift and unsupported and the organization with a weak spot that requires workaround and reduces efficiency.

Release of the employee: After due process and the application of robust performance management the employee exits the business.

Why Don't People Perform?

We believe that there are four reasons why people underperform.

A) They do not know what's expected of them
B) They don't know they are underperforming
C) They do not have the skills, ability, and equipment to do the job (i.e., they CAN'T)
D) The do not have the willingness or attitude to do the job (they WON'T).

The first two areas can be tackled through improved management of expectations. The last two areas can be managed using a skills–will matrix.

Managing Expectations

We need to open this section by saying that if you use a job map, and if you share that job map with your manager or member of staff then you minimize the risk of unclear expectations. So, our first piece of advice here is to use a job map. But the fact is that most managers don't do this and because of these unclear expectations sit at the heart of many performance issues. And here's why. Consider two circles connected like a Venn diagram. The circle on the left includes all the important aspects of your job as you see them. The circle on the right contains the important aspects of your job as your boss sees them. The shared area of the intersection contains aspects of your job that you both see as important.

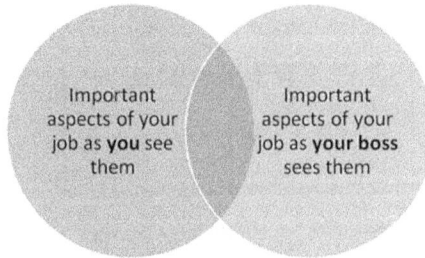

Now, in a relationship where expectations are clear and communication is good, the more the two circles can be pushed together, the greater is the shared area. The greater the shared area, the higher the shared expectation, the easier it might be to align goals and the firmer, I believe, are the foundations from which trust can develop. You simply understand each other a bit more.

Area of shared expectation is large

- Very closely aligned.
- Expectations are shared.
- Good alignment of goals.
- Good basis for trust.
- Probably feels successful.

But what if the circles only have a small area of shared expectation?

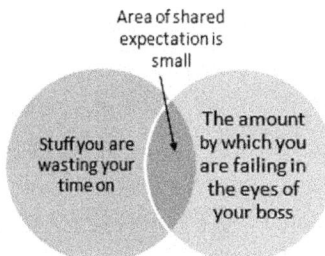

Area of shared expectation is small

Stuff you are wasting your time on

The amount by which you are failing in the eyes of your boss

- Poorly aligned.
- Few shared expectations.
- Poor alignment of goals.
- Poor basis for trust.
- Probably feel like giving up.

As you might imagine, this is not so good. Mutual understanding is poor, and expectations are not clear. Viewed from the perspective of the individual, the danger is that the things that remain outside the shared area in the left circle simply represent the amount of time that you are wasting on unimportant activities (as far as your boss is concerned). You should consider whether you need to convince your boss of the importance of these, and thereby bring them into the common ground, or stop doing them. What remains outside of the shared area in the right-hand zone is potentially even more dangerous, because it represents things that your boss thinks are an important part of your job but which you are not doing. In short, this is the degree to which you are failing in the eyes of your boss. Bad news indeed.

What needs to happen here? Well, in short, the expectation exchange becomes important again. As the manager you need to be sure that your staff know what's expected of them, otherwise you are simply setting them up to fail. And when they fail, so do you. It's easier to build trust when the circles are closer together. Clear expectations bring people together and make a firm foundation for the building of trust and managing performance.

Can't Do Versus Won't Do

The "Skills–Will Matrix" (also known as the "Ability/Willingness Matrix") is a tool introduced by Max Landsberg in his book *The Tao of Coaching*. Typically used to manage underperformance, the matrix can be used to help identify personal development strategies for even the most capable individuals and is a guide to choosing the best management or influencing style to guide staff members to success. It is helpful as a method to understand whether individuals have a skills issue that prevents them from performing in their role, which can be addressed through training and development, or a willingness or attitudinal issue which can be more about personal motivation and therefore can be harder to address.

The matrix requires an assessment to be made of an individual's level of skill or ability for dealing with a situation, issue, or task and also their level of willingness to take it on. The degree of skill someone has depends on their relevant knowledge, experience, training, and understanding. The amount of willingness someone has is more complex but is influenced, among other things, by the individual's desire to achieve and their attitudes toward incentives, security, confidence, the role, the business, the manager, and the team.

The Skills-Will Matrix

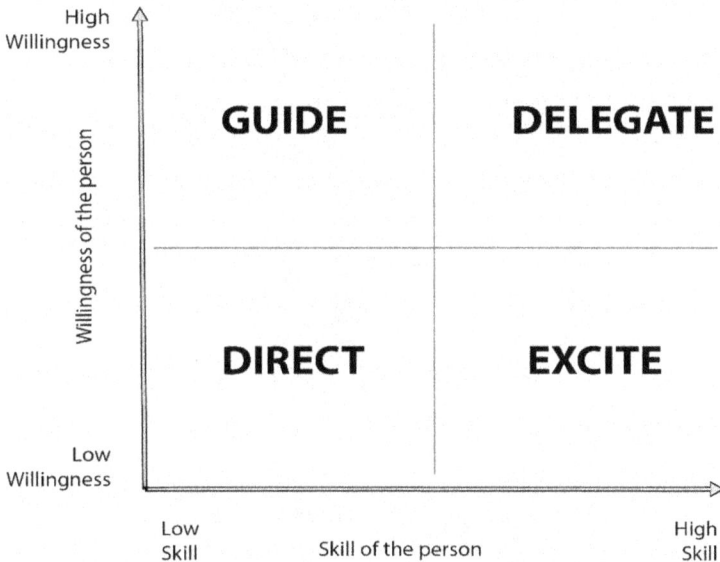

from Landsberg: The Tao of Coaching

Getting Better Outcomes for People with Low Willingness and Low Skill: DIRECT THEM

When the assessment of skill and willingness is low there is a need to develop both and to closely supervise the individual. To achieve this, you must firstly build the will. Then raise the skill. Then sustain the will. To build the will, the manager should provide the individual with a clear briefing. The individual should know exactly what is required of them for the particular situation, job, or task. It is important to identify the individual's motivations so that the manager can tap into these. Developing a vision of future performance with the individual can often help the coach to build the will. An individual who has a clear picture of how their future performance can be improved will be more likely to apply themselves to the situation at hand. The main method of skill development is through training and the manager should help the individual to identify where and when they can get the appropriate training and fully discuss opportunities for development. These may be on-the-job learning from peers through to formal training programs. If possible, this should be done as part of a Personal Development Plan with input from a learning and development professional. Other possibilities to include here are job swaps, placements, and sabbaticals. In addition, the manager can structure tasks for the individual to help them achieve quick wins, helping to develop confidence as well as skill. Sustaining the will comes about through regular one-to-one review sessions, open conversations, taking opportunities to develop trust, and encouraging a culture where the individual is encouraged to share ideas in an environment where those ideas are given a sensible hearing and developed where possible. Close monitoring is important to ensure that there is no return to old habits and managers must be clear that they share responsibility for fostering a motivational culture that allows team members to develop their own roles to maximize their job satisfaction opportunities.

Getting Better Outcomes for High Willingness and Low Skill: GUIDE THEM

Where there is a will, there is a way. The individual with high willingness and low skill already has the motivation to deal with the challenges they face. The main objective for the manager is therefore to help the individual develop the necessary skills required to improve performance. Once again, the key to skills development is often training and the role of the manager is to help the individual access the training they require. However, training does not necessarily involve simply going on a traditional course. Other and often better options could include the individual observing someone with the appropriate skills and experience or setting a series of smaller tasks to build up their skills gradually. Typical people found in this sector of the matrix include new staff, who have high willingness but who do not yet have all the skills they need to perform. A good induction process, one-to-one development reviews, and a well-structured plan to deliver skills development are essential. A personal development plan can also help. Remember that if the individual does not have their skills development needs met then they are at risk of becoming disengaged and their willingness may fall, dropping them into the DIRECT box.

Getting Better Outcomes for High Skill but Low Willingness: EXCITE THEM

This person has all the skills they need to do the job, so this situation is an exercise in motivation. The manager has to first identify the reason for the low will. This requires careful research and conversation. For example, the individual may be put off by the task and require help in seeing the personal benefit in carrying it out, or they may feel aggrieved over past events. Alternatively, there may be some demotivation due to the management style being adopted. Whatever the reason behind the lack of will, the role of the manager is to help the individual to identify actions that can be taken to improve the situation. Solutions need to be flexible, practical, and show early wins to maintain momentum. Positive feedback and encouragement, while important at all levels, is even more essential here.

Getting Better Outcomes for High Skill and High Willingness: DELEGATE TO THEM

Delegation is a hugely important skill in any manager's toolbox. It's a smart thing to learn how to do and all the best managers are good at it. Delegating works on three levels. Firstly, it develops others. Secondly, it means that you can get work off your plate, and, thirdly, it increases overall organizational resilience through the fact that there is no single point of failure (i.e., more than one person can handle the task being delegated). Individuals in this category of the matrix, highly skilled and highly motivated, are probably your stars and are often the easiest to manage, but this does not mean their needs are any less important. Potential for development remains high and the role of a manager in respect of someone whose skill and will are both high is to provide them with a sounding board and to develop their confidence to deal with new challenges. You must allow them to climb their work-based Maslow (see the Leadership chapter). The manager can help the individual set objectives but help with the method for achieving those objectives if often not required as the person is already well motivated.

The challenge for the manager in this situation is to work with the individual to set more challenging goals and to step back and let them get on with it. Although the individual is equipped with the necessary skills and motivation to be successful when dealing with a situation or task, the manager should still provide them with the appropriate feedback and praise.

If you've read the chapter on leadership, you will see strong areas of overlap between the matrix and the situational leadership model. As with those leadership areas, the essential aspect is one of our main themes that runs through this book: You can get the best out of others by changing your behavior to get the best out of them. It is about understanding the other people. By using the Skills–Will matrix, managers can effectively prepare for a successful relationship that develops motivated, engaged, and high-performing staff. It can be used with considerable practical success and supports a structured approach to managing high performance and for identifying and tackling underperformance. Managing performance is not rocket science. The best results come when well-trained and effective managers motivate and lead their teams to succeed, using a variety of techniques. The key to it all is building a business in which a positive, supportive, and professional culture allows people to be the best that they can be.

Remember These Golden Rules about Outcomes

EVERYBODY'S job has a key output. It's the reason their job exists.

JOB MAPS are a great tool for generating meaningful understanding about a job and the outcomes we expect from it.

You can use your job map to set SMART goals and objectives.

Having CLEAR expectations minimizes the risk of underperformance and allows people to create best outcomes.

You can use the SKILLS–WILL matrix to manage performance of all staff—not just those who are underperforming

CHAPTER 6

D Is for Decisions

Can You Make the Decisions That Lead to Success?

"Nothing is more difficult, and therefore more precious, than to be able to decide"

—Napoleon Bonaparte

Decision making is the process of selection and commitment to a purpose or a plan of action. It is a psychological process in which the decision maker chooses between various alternatives with the intent of reaching a maximal number of goals, while avoiding damage and unnecessary risks, and by using a minimal amount of resources. Studies of how we make decisions stretch back to Aristotle and Plato. A fine heritage indeed! In modern times decision making is defined as the "process of selection of and commitment to a purpose or plan of action" (Noorderhaven 1995) and is a key part of organizational life. It is accepted in modern times that decisions are made in the immediate short-term and long-term perspectives and that decision making can take different forms. You and I make decisions every day, subject to a number of biases and perceptions about the world. Organizations form committees to make decisions and devolve authority to individual managers whose role it is to make decisions. For managers this is an absolutely key part of organizational life. Managers see themselves as decision makers working in organizations and businesses which are designed, operated, and perceived as decision-making activities.

As anyone who has studied it will tell you, economics is all about decision making. The first thing that many economists learn about their mission is the study of the allocation of scarce resources. Central to the economic theories is the concept of *Homo economicus* or "Economic man," a person that acts at all times with perfect knowledge to maximize the most efficient economic outcome. He (all the texts tend to refer to this being as a he) applies a strictly rational basis to decision making. He weighs up the pros and cons carefully in each case before making his decision. He has good—often perfect—intelligence. He has good information about the world around in which to make decisions. He will always follow a "decision tree" to achieve the optimal outcome which, since he has perfect knowledge, he will have identified from the outset. Such thinking is at the heart of most microeconomic theories around organizational behavior, but, over time, has been increasingly and successfully critiqued. Any interpretation of available literature will expose a modern consensus in support of a realization that *Homo economicus* does not exist, but that such a being is conceptually acceptable as a simplification of the real world around which economic study can be made.

The key theories of rational decision making (also termed Traditional Decision-Making Theory—or Normative Decision Making) stem from a behavioral or cognitive science perspective developed from the works of Simon (1957), March and Simon (1958), and Cyert and March (1963). These models were developed to help decision makers cope with uncertainty. The process that underpins them is typically built around defining a problem, identifying relevant criteria dimensions of the problem, and weighing those criteria in terms of importance to enable the decision maker to generate a range of alternative solutions that address the problem. As mentioned earlier, this often involves the creation of a decision tree to allow options to be selected, rating each alternative before choosing the optimal solution. This concept of process in respect to decision making is a common theme in descriptions of the rational model. Such "decision tree" models are normative in as much as they suggest what the decision maker should do, as opposed to what he or she actually does.

The rational view describes a consistency in the relationship between cause and effect that many more modern-day scholars might challenge. Rationalists like Adair (1985) and Moore and Thomas (1988) might suggest that the basic stages of decision making are focused on the key aspects of understanding and structuring the problem, assessing the uncertainties and the possible outcomes, and determining the optional strategy. This three-stage process (or five as Adair puts it) suggests that decision making is a linear process with a form of optimization that is consciously selected by the decision maker. It is this aspect that has been most significantly challenged in the past 15 years.

So, what?

Such normative approaches may be excellent if you are trying to determine whether to spend a billion pounds on a bridge or an airport, but such models fit less comfortably when discussing how decisions are actually made in the lived experience of individuals where such steps are not consciously possible due to the range of stressors involved. In these situations, we rely on something else. The question is, what?

On an individual level, our approach toward decision making can be looked at in terms of our preference for information, our ability to apply "gut feel," and our approach to risk. For many of us, decision making is problematic. We like to think that we weigh up all the pros and cons of a situation before making a decision. The facts only make up part of the picture, but we pursue them as far as we can and like them to be at the basis of our decision making. After all, a decision made without any facts is just a hunch, right? Well, maybe. But when it comes to organizational decision making, where decisions are scrutinized and assessed after the event is right or wrong, then we tend to attempt (or at least to show) that we are applying a rational process of weighing up a situation and making decision based on those inputs.

But for some managers decision making can be a block, especially where we feel that we do not have enough information.

There are some crucial characteristics of good decision making that we see in the businesses we work with. They can be summarized as follows:

1. They focus on the future, not the past
2. They do not make knee-jerk decisions made without reference to the perceived facts
3. The best decision makers know when to break free from analysis paralysis
4. The decision is communicated clearly and reasons are given
5. The decision is followed through. It is reviewed and reflected upon at a future point and the learning applied

The Problem–Reason–Solution Loop

Decisions commonly need to be made to counter a PROBLEM. Something has gone wrong, and a decision has to be made. This is a common situation for a manager in any business. An e-mail, a conversation in a corridor, the report from a subordinate, a red line on a report can all flag to us that a situation has arisen that is creating a variance from the desired situation, and we need to act accordingly. Consider the department manager reviewing his budget report and seeing he is overbudget in one area by 20 percent. What does she do?

In the first instance the manager looks for a REASON that has created the problem. This situation must have come about as a direct consequence of something that had happened. What was it? The reason might be straightforward (maybe she blew a big chunk of budget on one expensive trip) or it might be very complex where no precise cause is visible on initial enquiry. So, what does the manager do? Well most commonly they will ask for more information in an attempt to uncover the reason behind the situation. In every good manager is a detective struggling to get out. This detective welcomes a break from the stresses of being at the sharp end of decision making and agenda setting and loves the forensics attached to delving deeper and deeper into a problem to get to the root cause. This propensity for detail is fascinating, and we allow it on the basis that such a review will inform our situation and enable us to understand the detail behind the dilemma. Because knowing the detail adds to my knowledge, and it enables the manager to speak knowledgably about the situation at the next managers' meeting. They feel good because they know that they have got to the bottom of the situation, and knowledge is something that gives us power.

So, time spent on analysis is a good thing? The question mark in that sentence is important, because the answer is not straightforward. The difficult thing for many managers to remember is that when they embark on a detective journey into the facts, their forward momentum in other areas can be lost. Lots of clichés come into play here, each one counteracting the next. Not to learn from history is to repeat the mistakes we made in the past, to understand the future one needs to understand the past, etc., are all valid. But there is a reason the windshield is larger than the rearview mirror. It is crucially important that the manager keeps sight of where the team is going, not on where they have been.

There is therefore a compromise to be made. Yes, it is important that I spend some time indulging that inner detective and completing that forensic examination but only up to a point. While I am analyzing the past I become fearful of making decisions on the future. The manager in the example above is unlikely to approve the next spend request until she understands the issue that created the problem. She becomes focused in the past and not on the future. This is a bad place to spend too much time. There is a great problem-solving approach called the 5-whys. It is proposed by many as a great way to get to the *root? or route?* cause of issues. And it is a great method. Why is this budget line 20 percent overspent? Because the flagship project needed a 3-day client meeting not the 2 days normally required. Why did it take 3 days and not 2? Because the client wasn't happy with progress on the roll-out. Why wasn't the client happy with the roll-out? Because the specialist accounting submodule that formed part of the core package was not working as expected. Why was that submodule not working properly? Because the team working on the module did not have a programmer qualified in the relevant language. Bingo. What started off as a budget issue turns out to be a resource issue. Now the manager is in a position to make a decision and should do so rapidly.

We kid ourselves that before embarking on a big decision that we must first define the problem. The tough thing is that it is hard to know where to draw the line. The issue is that this analysis merely opens up another can of worms. On how many other projects is this an issue? Why did we not know that this issue had arisen? Is the project manager utilizing his resources in the best way? Will we have to revise our cost schedules on all other projects? Do we need to think about using another module instead where we have greater competence? The list of questions can go on and on. And congratulations by the way, because while you have been asking yourself all these questions, you have just entered the world of analysis paralysis, that indecisive state of mind where you don't know what to do for the best, because where you thought you just had one problem (this project is overspent by 20 percent), you now realize that you actually have 100 other problems. And boy, does that weigh you down. Mentally this is a tough place to be. Instead of feeling good because you have identified the reason for a problem, you feel bad because you have unveiled a whole load more stuff that will now keep you awake at night. This is the lived reality of organizational decision making; it is all too easy to allow yourself to be drawn into a state of analysis paralysis, where your main efforts and concerns are drawn into a deeper and deeper review of the situation, and you become less focused on defining the way ahead. So that request for future spend sits on your desk waiting to be reviewed. And the longer you spend analyzing the problem and the deeper you go into your probing, the harder it is to get out. There are some great books on the traps of decision making, including Russo and Schoemaker's book *Decision Traps* and David Wethey's excellent and highly readable *Decide*.

For problem-based decision making it is essential that you go around the loop from PROBLEM to REASON. This makes absolute sense. To go straight from PROBLEM to SOLUTION would be to carelessly neglect the root cause of the issue. But you must not get stuck in the analysis–paralysis loop.

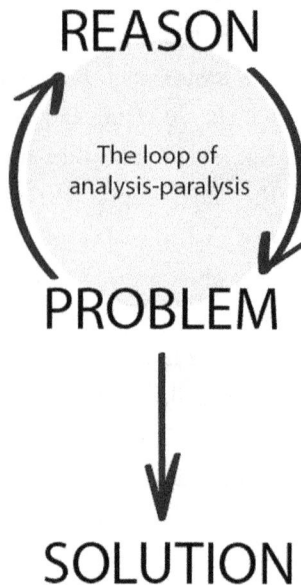

REASON

The loop of
analysis-paralysis

PROBLEM

SOLUTION

To make good decisions you must know when problem solving ends and decision making starts. Of course, the way that we analyze and view these decisions isn't actually rational at all. We are all prone to bias, which means our decisions are often constructed on poor grounds. Sometimes there is simply too much information coming at us in one go. This can swamp us and instantly put us into paralysis mode. Imagine every double-glazing salesperson in the country knocking on your door at the same time. The noise, the propositions, and the sheer overwhelming nature of the information being provided would make it almost impossible to make a rational and correct decision about which product to buy. So, what do we do? We sift out information that we deem as irrelevant or wrong and opt to support outcomes that we are predisposed toward, or which reinforce our own views of the world. For a start, we tend to believe in and agree with people who are more like us. This means we close out those who are not, even if they have the better product. In addition, we are heavily influenced by the first information we receive, judging all others against that criteria because that was the information checkpoint against which all other information can be assessed. The hard truth is that in business you have to make decisions based on little or, sometimes, no information. For most of us this is scary. In the example we have described, the manager needs to make decision on the future spend request before he or she has the answer to the 5-whys. This is risky, but it is the only way to move the business forward. This is hard, and I mean REALLY hard for many managers, and as consultants we commonly work with businesses and teams who can feel stuck in the analysis–paralysis loop. The key thing is that you must retain a future focus and you must break out of the PROBLEM to REASON loop and burst into SOLUTION mode.

This requires an action-oriented mindset. Problem solving is rearward looking. Decision making is about what WILL happen in the future. The trouble is that the future is not certain.

There are lots of activity and process going on around the outside of our decision making that have a key role to play in how our decisions plan out. These form the heart of what the great Prussian military thinker Carl von Clausewitz defined as "friction." Friction is composed of three gaps: the knowledge gap—the difference between what we know and what we don't know; the alignment gap—the difference between what we want people to do and what they actually do; and the effects gap—the difference between the outcomes that we expect to happen and what actually happens. The basic crux of what Clausewitz says (to paraphrase a huge thought leader in just a few words) was that the world is uncertain, and that these gaps will always be there. The best decision makers and leaders recognize that and just get on with it!

We must accept that there is a gap in our knowledge, and that the actions we choose may not have the outcomes we expect, and that people might not always do exactly what we expect of them. Our ability to make sense of this complex environment comes down to our ability to recognize patterns, and in establishing links between cause and effect. If you believe that the greatest indicator of future performance is past performance, then you'd probably be right most of the time. But if it is that easy then we would be able to predict the winner of the next horse race just by reviewing the last races run by those horses. In reality we know that while we might be able to predict—individually and without interference from the others—how each individual horse will perform, we never know for sure until we get them out on the track. The way the horses interact, the state of the ground, the combination of straights and bends all make it hard for us to predict, not to mention throwing different jockeys into the mix. Decision making is about recognizing that those gaps and uncertainties exist and doing it anyway. A decision that is 80 percent right is better than no decision at all.

This is where the emotional side to our decision making must come in. Our rational approach (which, don't forget, isn't rational anyway) sits on top of our emotional intuition rather like a blanket. Our emotional intuition actually underlays our rational framework. We choose things that are "rational" based on how we define and experience the world. Those views are emotional and shaped by our upbringing, values, ethos, beliefs, and the many other aspects of deep psychology. As briefly outlined earlier, as humans we are inherently prejudiced and biased. And we can some-times feel when something is "right" or "wrong." We call this "intuition." Intuition is not something we are born with. For sure it is something that grows and develops over the years and is shaped by our experiences and life history. Intuitive decision making means quickly getting under the surface of a situation and making sense of it in a way that allows us to see how different course of actions might influence it. Intuitive decision makers rely on gut feel.

Understanding the reasons behind your decision making is very important as they can reveal some of the assumptions that you hold to be true. Insightful learning can come from the review of these assumptions. This is especially useful when attempting to form strategy, when our decisions are often based on a personal view of the world that may or may not be true. By analyzing these assumptions, we can ask ourselves—is that *really* true? And by this we can keep our thinking fresh and be sure that we are testing our decisions for signs of bias and prejudicial thinking.

Exercise: Think about a problem you are facing and apply the 5-whys model to understand more about it. Write the problem here.

What factors are affecting your perception of the problem?

What does your 5-why's analysis tell you about the problem?

What would be the implication of NOT making a decision?

Now make your decision—what will you DO to overcome the problem based on your 5-why analysis (resist the temptation to revisit your problem analysis).

Making Better Decisions More Quickly

Typically, decision making is about closing the gap between where we are and where we want to be. Once we decide, we act. After acting, we monitor the results of our actions. Finally, we evaluate the results we've monitored. This can be presented as a Decision Cycle like the one shown below:

The Decision Cycle

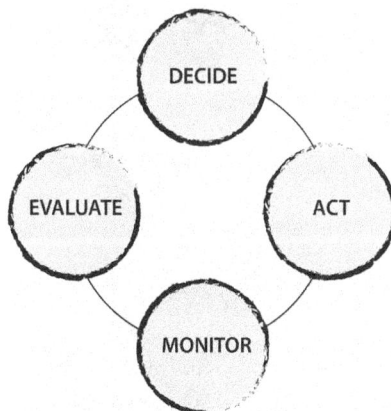

This loop is familiar to us and many of us will recognize this as being valid for most organizations. We make a decision, we act on it, we monitor what happens, and we evaluate the outcome. Its simplicity is central to its success, but to throw a different light on this I want to introduce the concept of a similar but subtly different model for understanding decision making in action and explain how fast decision making can keep you one step ahead of your competition. I want to introduce you to the OODA loop.

The OODA Loop

One of the most interesting and fascinatingly simple models in the study of how people actually make decisions is a model called the OODA Loop. The loop originated from Colonel John Boyd of the US Air Force who originally proposed it as a way of explaining how fighter pilots in the Korean War were able to outperform their communist opponents with such apparent ease and regularity, even though the communists were in technically superior aircraft like the superb MiG jet fighter. The consequent theory became hugely popular and remains one of the cornerstones of military doctrine and "heat of the moment" decision making. The loop also has application to the business world, as we shall see.

The OODA Loop

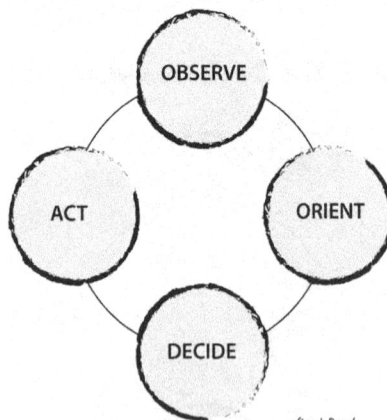

after J. Boyd

The loop as described by Boyd involves four actions—Observe, Orient, Decide, and Act—occurring in a sequenced process that, when completed more rapidly than the opponent, allow the pilot the opportunity of seizing the initiative in the complex and changing environment of a critical incident or dogfight. The principle of the loop from a military perspective is that the faster a decision maker can make his way around the loop, the more likely he is to stay one step ahead of his enemy.

Observe is about awareness. It is the unfolding situational data that is reaching the manager. This is sensual awareness and relates to both the external world outside of you and the internal world of what is going on within you (yes, feelings are data).

Orient, the next factor, becomes the basis for decision and action. It is here that we assimilate the data that is generated by observation. Thus, it is not simply what we see but how our training, background, and experiences allow us to create a contextualized story about what is going on. As Boyd described it:

> Without our genetic heritage, cultural traditions, and previous experiences, we do not possess an implicit repertoire of psychological skills shaped by environments and changes that have been previously experienced.

In other words, we apply our own patterns and experience to what we see, which influences our interpretation. Thus, orient becomes the lens through which we view the situation. This is where we bring ourselves and all our history, knowledge, and bias (conscious or otherwise) to the situation. It includes our values and beliefs, and the application of our own intuition. As the US Marines have it:

> We should base our decisions on awareness rather than on mechanical habit. That is, we act on a keen appreciation for the essential factors that make each situation unique instead of from conditioned response . . . since all decisions must be made in the face of uncertainty and since every situation is unique, there is no perfect solution to any battlefield problem. Therefore, we should not agonize over one. The essence of the problem is to select a promising course of action with an acceptable degree of risk and to do it more quickly than our foe. In this respect, "a good plan violently executed now is better than a perfect plan executed next week"
> —Warfighting—US Marine Doctrine (1997)

These internal models and paradigms are forever being recreated, analyzed, and assessed. It might be argued then that there exists a subloop within the main loop where our own orientation is being constantly reappraised through an internal process of reflection and reappraisal. As the person works their way around the loop they reassess their situation against these eternally developing paradigms and schemas that are influential in guiding the formation of a hypothesis and thus guiding them toward making a decision.

This suggestion of hypothesis generation as a key part of decision making is supported by Gary Klein's work. Klein, a widely published and much respected voice in the field of naturalistic decision making, argues that experts have highly tuned senses of intuition formed by extensive experience and enabling them to identify early onset of certain situations, or to spot the errors in apparently novel solutions.

In his Recognition Primed Decision-Making model, Klein argues that they are more able to identify patterns to an event or situation. As such, within the orientation phase of the loop, they are more able to apply some form of pattern match that allows them to select a "best outcome" hypothesis in the decide phase of the loop.

Where this process of pattern matching turns up a blank, then we have knowledge gap. A subsequent decision then may not have such clear outcomes, but the data generated by observing the outcomes arising from the actions will be analyzed and form part of the subsequent orient phase. Thus, where there is a mismatch between intended and subsequent outcome, the expert is more able to observe and orient the new data, coming potentially to a better solution more rapidly than the novice.

Decisions then are the manifestation of the early two factors, which Boyd also referred to as the finalized hypothesis. This is where the manager really has an opportunity to influence the outcome, using the data and understandings of it that have been gathered in the first two stages to decide upon a course of action.

The final stage is the action stage, where the decisions are put into effect. In well-oiled organizations the time taken between decision and action will be low. Inertia at this stage, especially in rapidly changing situations, can have a seriously detrimental effect, paralyzing the organization and creating more problems than solutions.

How Do You Apply It?

Quite simply the faster you can go around the loop the more able you will be to influence events, and stay one step ahead of the competition. Boyd identified this as being essential in retaining the initiative in an aerial dogfight, but the applications to business are obvious. The faster you can process the loop, the more opportunities there are for information acquisition and data processing through observation and orientation. These will lead to more opportunities for decision making and the creation of novel solutions and opportunities to drive the agenda. Your opponent or competitor must react to what you do. This puts him on the back foot.

But while your own capabilities might be great, it is the relative ability of your competitor to go through the same process that will have the most significant impact. If he is able to go around his loop faster than you are able to go around yours, then he is more able to claim the initiative, and create events to which you can only react. No matter how hard you try, he will always have the capacity to be "inside your loop," better able to influence the outcome of the contest in his favor. In a nutshell, he is more likely to win.

Linking to Intuition—"Trust Your Feelings"

We've all seen it. It's one of the most famous cinema sequences of all time. Luke Skywalker is hurtling at high speed along the narrow canyon around the middle of *The Death Star*. On his shoulders rests the last hope for the rebellion. If he succeeds in targeting his torpedo on the tiny exhaust port target, then the explosion it creates will cause a chain reaction that will lead to the destruction of the Empire's most deadly weapon. Skywalker will be a hero and his friends will live. Should he fail, his friends will suffer a terrible fate and the rebel base will be destroyed, plunging the galaxy into endless torment and suffering at the hands of the evil Emperor and his even more sinister minions.

Tough call.

Skywalker is piloting a state-of-the-art spaceship, crammed with targeting systems and computer-guided what-nots designed by experts to maximize the chances of the all-important direct hit. Others have tried to hit the exhaust port before him, but all have failed. Now, with the fate of the galaxy resting on his actions, Skywalker switches off the computer.

"Trust your feelings, Luke."

The eerie voice of his mentor Obi-Wan Kenobi gives the young Jedi the faith he needs to deliver success. When it comes down to it, at the final moment, Skywalker looks within himself and finds the inner courage and emotional intuition to obtain the best outcome.

It is the Skywalker moment.

And it's fiction.

Or is it?

In organizations, and in the world of management, there are times when we know that we have to turn our back on left brain logic. There are times when we have to turn off that big data targeting computer. There are times when we have to let go and trust our feelings, relying instead on our own gut instincts, our internal compass or whatever you want to call it. As the upper-class twit in the old Croft sherry TV advert used to say, "One instinctively knows when something is right."

I'm not saying that we should use "The Force" to guide management decisions (well, not openly at least), but we know that there are times when the Skywalker moment surges up inside of us. But when it does we don't always feel able to let go. All that computer logic is hard to turn our back on. Imagine if we could switch off the metaphorical targeting computer and challenge the established logic. This of course takes courage and leaves us feeling exposed. So we tend to avoid it. But we don't have to. We can learn to listen to our inner self and question the logic. We can learn to use our feelings as data and in so doing perhaps we can enhance our chances of selecting the best possible course of action.

So next time you are hurtling at high speed around your own personal death star listen out for the data that your feelings are providing to you. And trust them. Because intuitive decisions are not guesswork. They are based on much deeper processes.

The military make a split. They suggest that intuition-led decision making is most likely to be found closer to the front line, and that it will therefore be experienced most by more junior officers. They argue that further up the chain of command the process becomes more of an analytical and rational one where there may be a more obvious weighing up of the options. This is mirrored in Skywalker's story. At the sharp end, where the conditions are more uncertain and the consequences more immediately telling, the young Jedi knight applies a different form of intuitive and naturalistic decision making.

As the British Army puts it:

Intuition is a recognitive quality, based on military judgement, which in turn rests on an informed understanding of the situation based on professional knowledge and experience.

The Germans have a much better word for intuition in this context: *fingerspitzengefühl*, which means, quite literally, "fingertip feeling." It represents the sense that the most able commanders have to appraise the situation (Observe and Orient in OODA terms). It is about harnessing that gut instinct of what is going on even if you can't quite put your finger on exactly what that might be. Instead, you trust your feelings. The best commanders exhibit this tendency, and so do Jedi knights.

And so, we believe, do the best managers.

Remember These Golden Rules of Decision Making

There is no such thing as perfect knowledge. You will NEVER have all the information you need.

Sometimes you will have to decide between two options NEITHER of which you like or are perfect and then you must choose the least/worst option! It is hard being at the top.

Decision making isn't always rational. In fact, it rarely is. You must TRUST your feelings.

SPEED and INTENT count for something. A good plan violently executed NOW is better than a perfect plan executed next week.

BEWARE of the analysis–paralysis loop

References

Adair, J. 1985. *Effective Decision Making*. London: Pan Books.

Cyert, R.M., and J.G. March. 1963. *A Behavioral Theory of the Firm*. With contributions by G.P.E. Clarkson and others. Englewood Cliffs, NJ: Prentice-Hall.

March, J.G., and H.A. Simon. 1958. *Organisations*. New York: Wiley.

Moore, P.G. and Thomas, H. 1988. *The Anatomy of Decisions*. London: Penguin.

Nooderhaven, N. G. 1995. *Strategic Decision Making*. Wokingham, England: Addison Wesley.

Simon, H.A. 1957. *Models of Man Social and Rational: Mathematical Essays on Rational Human Behavior in a Social Setting*. New York: Wiley.

United States Marine Corps. 1997. *Warfighting*. Department of the Navy and U S Marine Corps. Washington DC, U.S. Government. PCN 142 000006 00

CHAPTER 7

Conclusions

"I am slowly coming to the conclusion that it's more important to learn to work with what you've got, under the circumstances you've been given, than wishing for different ones."

—Charlotte Eriksson

Sometimes we learn fast. Swing one punch and you'll make contact, but swing another and I'll duck. That's fast learning. But learning just why it was that you wanted to punch me in the first place takes a little longer. For that to happen I need to learn about you, I need to learn about me, and I need to learn what it is about our relationship that stimulates the Frank Bruno tendencies in you. Learning comes via action and learning from that action through the act of reflection.

Learning isn't always easy. It is often challenging. Ever heard the phrase "I learn most when I'm out of my comfort zone?" Well, it may be true, but life outside the comfort zone (and maybe I'll revisit just what a comfort zone is in another blog entry one day) comes with lots of other challenges that might actually restrict learning.

We are all on a learning journey. Learning starts as soon as a newborn baby learns how to breathe in air and stops, arguably, when we learn what it is to be dead. At all points in between we are weaving our learning journey. This journey can be enriched by learning how to learn, and this starts with a journey of self-discovery.

To misquote another famous saying: "To learn about others you must first learn about yourself." This has a ring of truth about it. Knowing our own preferences, bias, and strengths helps us to understand who we are, and helps us to understand how others see us. I accept that I am shaped by a lifetime of unique experiences and influences that make me different from you. My learning allows me to be confident in my own power, a sort of self-assurance and personal gravitas that has given me the ability to identify, stimulate, and pursue an inquiry. In our own experiences it has given us the opportunity, drive, and more importantly the courage to launch businesses. Most notably though it has given us the ability to finally know who we are as people, and to be comfortable with that. This is a prize that's been worthy of any investment made.

Now that you have read Blood, what final advice can we offer you as you embark on your continued journeys of self-development? Well we would love you to read the other books too. The second and third books in this trilogy, Sweat and Tears, explore ten further areas that, if mastered, will help grow your organization, your team, and your own skills as a manager or leader. But there are some important other aspects that you can start to do immediately and even before reading these other books.

Firstly, **accept yourself as data**. Your experiences are valid. The thoughts, feelings, and experiences that you have are yours and are real. Don't be dictated by others (and, yes, there is a certain irony in even writing that in a list of tips!). Take as much information as you can from situations. Reflection is a key tool. Assimilate your data, your thoughts, your feelings, your observations, your history, and turn it into learning. You know your strengths and your weaknesses—and seek feedback from others. Notice how your strengths and weaknesses and hopes and fears affect you and drive your choices. When important things happen, take time to notice your own feelings and responses. Notice the emotional responses and line of thought that it provokes. It's all data. Record these feelings. Junkies of this kind of thing use a reflective diary to capture all that stuff. It's not necessary, but some find it helpful.

Secondly, **do not fear change**, accept it as an opportunity to take action to live a diverse existence. Again, recognize your thoughts and feelings. Take note of the internal dialogue that goes on as you wrestle over decision making and fears of change. You can take learning from that. To develop is to change. It is in the nature of the journey.

Measure twice and cut once—it is always better to be safe than sorry.

Allow time for yourself. All of us, whether we are parents, children, husbands, wives, managers, coworkers, may sometimes feel blocked by the world around us. To learn is to accept that it is a perfectly normal and shared experience. Following your own learning path sometimes means that you have to be selfish. Don't be afraid to take some "me time" when you need to. Recognize and satisfy your own needs. For many of us this is not as easy as it sounds. It can be hard to be selfish when others need you. But sometimes you have to be hard. To learn is to develop an appropriate level of assertiveness to enable you to hold a space for what needs to be done. Use the SPECTRUM⁻ model to help you. It works.

Love what you do. And if you don't love it, don't do it. Lots of things will catch your eye, but only a few catch your heart. Pursue those, talk about them passionately, and indulge your time on them. At the same time expect all your employees to love what they do, it is ok to have fun at work. Even undertakers and funeral directors have fun at work.

If you don't know something, just ask. You can learn a lot about yourself through feedback from others. You'd be surprised how many people will give you honest feedback if you ask the right way. Good questions such as "What did you think of the way I did X?" or "I'd like to get better at Y ... could you suggest any changes I might make?" are all good ways of drawing out ideas from others. But then you must Listen. Listen to the responses that others give to you, and if you don't understand it, or if you feel it's unclear, then simply ask them to clarify. Often, and I think this is especially true in organizations, we build up fantasies about why other people do what they do, or what type of lives they have, or how they think. Sometimes we waste time tip-toeing softly around an issue that might not be real at all. You want to know if they think you're a good Project Manager? Just ask responsible questions. Step into your power. It sounds absurd, but its validity is proven.

Learn to be responsible. Sometimes we all feel that we can't get out of a situation. We might feel that things are being done to us to keep us in a less than perfect state. "I can't change that," for instance. Sometimes looking at it from a position of responsibility can help to determine a course of action. You can learn to change it.

Take a whole-system focus. It is easy to assume, through the safe and siloed approach of a book, that making changes in one area can take place independently and without impacting other areas. The real world, of course, is nothing like this. Changes in one area of your work will impact the other areas. Some of these impacts are obvious and predictable whereas others might be subtle, unpredictable, and, quite possibly, not apparent for some time. The crucial thing is to realize and accept the connected nature of all things. Making a big change in one area can have an amplified effect on another area, for good or for bad. Big changes, unless they are fundamentally essential, are best avoided. They feel messy and are hard to maintain. In most cases, small adjustments of behavior have the best outcomes. We often ask clients to think of their skills base as though they were a DJ with a mixing desk. Making small adjustments here and there maximizes the quality of output from even the roughest of basic instruments. Fine tuning your own performance using the mixing desk of skills in this book can make for a virtuoso performance worthy of a standing ovation.

You have just read Book One in the trilogy *Blood, Sweat, and Tears*. We hope that you enjoyed it, and that you will go on to further improve your mixing desk of skills by reading Book Two, *Sweat*, and Book Three, *Tears*.

Index

OTHER TITLES IN THE ENTREPRENEURSHIP AND SMALL BUSINESS MANAGEMENT COLLECTION

Scott Shane, Case Western University, *Editor*

- *African American Entrepreneurs: Successes and Struggles of Entrepreneurs of Color in America* by Michelle Ingram Spain and J. Mark Munoz
- *How to Get Inside Someone's Mind and Stay There: The Small Business Owner's Guide to Content Marketing and Effective Message Creation* by Jacky Fitt
- *Profit: Plan for It, Get It—The Entrepreneurs Handbook* by H.R. Hutter
- *Navigating Entrepreneurship: 11 Proven Keys to Success* by Larry Jacobson
- *Global Women in the Start-up World: Conversations in Silicon Valley* by Marta Zucker
- *Understanding the Family Business: Exploring the Differences Between Family and Nonfamily Businesses, Second Edition* by Keanon J. Alderson
- *Growth-Oriented Entrepreneurship* by Alan S. Gutterman
- *Founders* by Alan S. Gutterman
- *Entrepreneurship* by Alan S. Gutterman
- *Sustainable Entrepreneurship* by Alan S. Gutterman
- *Startup Strategy Humor: Democratizing Startup Strategy* by Rajesh K. Pillania
- *Can You Run Your Business With Blood, Sweat, and Tears? Volume II: Sweat* by Stephen Elkins-Jarrett and Nick Skinner
- *Can You Run Your Business With Blood, Sweat, and Tears? Volume III: Tear* by Stephen Elkins-Jarrett and Nick Skinner

Announcing the Business Expert Press Digital Library

Concise e-books business students need for classroom and research

This book can also be purchased in an e-book collection by your library as

- a one-time purchase,
- that is owned forever,
- allows for simultaneous readers,
- has no restrictions on printing, and
- can be downloaded as PDFs from within the library community.

Our digital library collections are a great solution to beat the rising cost of textbooks. E-books can be loaded into their course management systems or onto students' e-book readers.

The **Business Expert Press** digital libraries are very affordable, with no obligation to buy in future years. For more information, please visit **www.businessexpertpress.com/librarians**. To set up a trial in the United States, please email **sales@businessexpertpress.com**.

www.ingramcontent.com/pod-product-compliance
Lightning Source LLC
Chambersburg PA
CBHW062042200326
41519CB00017B/5102